SPEAKING OF
ℳIRACLES

SPEAKING OF *MIRACLES*

The Faith Experience at the Basilica of the National Shrine of Saint Ann in Scranton, Pennsylvania

FR. CASSIAN J. YUHAUS, CP,
WITH FR. RICHARD FRECHETTE, CP

PAULIST PRESS
New York • Mahwah, NJ

Cover design by Lynn Else
Book design by ediType

Photographs by Harold W. James III Studio, Somerville, NJ.

Library of Congress Cataloging-in-Publication Data

Yuhaus, Cassian J.
    Speaking of miracles : the faith experience at the Basilica of the
National Shrine of Saint Ann in Scranton, Pennsylvania / Cassian J.
Yuhaus ; with Richard Frechette.
        p.   cm.
    Includes bibliographical references.
    ISBN 0-8091-4447-6 (alk. paper)
    1. Basilica of the National Shrine of Saint Ann (Scranton, Pa.) –
History. 2. Scranton (Pa.) – Church history.   I. Frechette, Richard.
II. Title.
BX4603.S62Y84 2007
282′.74837 – dc22

                                                2006010530

Published by Paulist Press
997 Macarthur Boulevard
Mahwah, New Jersey 07430

www.paulistpress.com

Printed and bound in the
United States of America

To the Mothers and Fathers
the Grandmothers and Grandfathers
that long line of
true friends and devotees of St. Ann
who have made these grounds holy
and have experienced miraculous responses
to their prayers and petitions.
They have given to their children
what they cherished most —
the fullness of our Catholic Faith
and a true devotion to our Special Patron,
Good St. Ann.

CONTENTS

Photographs follow page 96.

BASILICA PRAYER

Lord God,
to the greater glory of your Holy Name
and
for increased blessing and healing
upon
the thousands of faithful who come here,
listen to
Our Basilica Prayer.
Bless our families, bless our children,
heal our sick, comfort our afflicted,
bless our homes.
Hear the prayer of all who come here
from near and far away
to glorify your name with us,
to sing your praises
and
to offer thanks for the blessings received
through the intercession of our Passionist Saints,
and in particular through the help of
our Glorious Patron,
St. Ann.

FOREWORD

Dear Friends and Devotees of St. Ann,

Our late Holy Father, the Servant of God Pope John Paul II, has conferred a great honor on all of you in elevating St. Ann's Monastery Shrine to the dignity and honor of a minor Basilica for the entire Church. Since this blessing is in perpetuity, I am certain that our present Holy Father, Pope Benedict XVI, who knows the Passionists well from his visits to them in Germany, reaffirms that special blessing.

I recall with great joy my first visit to your beautiful shrine in October 1993, at the invitation of my dear friend and collaborator Fr. Cassian J. Yuhaus, CP, who was at that time rector of the Monastery Community and Director of the Shrine. I remember well that evening when after the Solemn Liturgy at 8:00 p.m., I stood in line until midnight to receive the hundreds of faithful people, young and older, who wanted to share with me their faith experience on the holy grounds of this National Shrine to St. Ann. I was convinced even then of the worthiness of St. Ann's to be raised to the dignity and honor of a Basilica. Basilicas are eminently places of extraordinary faith, devotion, and worship.

I was very happy to learn that Fr. Cassian, together with Fr. Rick Frechette, CP, has gathered your testimonials in order to make them available to all the faithful so that together we may thank God for all the extraordinary blessings bestowed on us through the intercession of the grandmother of Jesus, the mother of Mary, good St. Ann.

I was privileged to celebrate Eucharist with you at the Monastery Shrine before reconstruction began. I was overjoyed to preside at a special Liturgy for the solemn dedication of the Basilica on October 18, 1997, the eve of the feast of St. Paul of the Cross. I was very honored to concelebrate that Liturgy with His Excellency Bishop James C. Timlin, Bishop of Scranton, whose devotion to St. Ann and whose love for the Passionists were evident as he inaugurated and carried through the process for Basilica status.

I have followed the work you have done over these many years. I congratulate you and all the many friends and benefactors of St. Ann's who have made all this possible. I know of the laudable ministries the Passionists fulfill not only at St. Ann's but throughout the United States and, in fact, throughout the world. Your beautiful sanctuary of St. Gabriel at Gran Sasso is well known to us. St. Gabriel's attracts several million people on pilgrimage and prayer each year and is a source of many blessings.

It is my hope that St. Ann's will see a similar increase in faith and devotion so that the prayers of all who come to this holy place will be answered.

I thank Fr. Cassian and Fr. Rick for putting this fine book together for all to enjoy. The early history of St. Ann's is amazing. I thank Fr. Charles Connor, Ph.D., for his excellent research. I was very pleased to see the emphasis on the dogmatic foundation and the strong insistence on the sacredness of the family and indeed of all life.

I implore my blessing upon all who come to increase their faith experience at the beautiful Basilica of the National Shrine of St. Ann.

With sentiments of regard and esteem, I am fraternally in Christ,

ACHILLE CARDINAL SILVESTRINI, D.D.
Vatican City, July 2006

PREFACE

It was a delight and an honor to welcome to our diocese His Eminence and my dear friend Achille Cardinal Silvestrini in October 1993 for what turned out to be a very significant visit. His Eminence knew about St. Ann's through his friendship with the Passionists in Rome and in the United States. While accomplishing other tasks pertaining to his high office at the Vatican, he made it a point to clear his schedule so that he could see for himself what was the faith experience at the National Shrine of St. Ann in Scranton, Pennsylvania. He was not disappointed. Hundreds of people spoke to him about their personal experience of faith and devotion at our shrine. Days afterward His Eminence shared with me his conviction that St. Ann's was indeed a unique and distinctive place where God's favor and blessing is manifest in the lives of so very many faithful who seek the intercession of our beloved patron, St. Ann. He expressed his personal conviction that St. Ann's had all the qualifications requisite to have this holy place elevated to the honor and the dignity of a Basilica. I assured His Eminence that his conviction had been mine of many years prior to his welcome October visit. It was this exchange that prompted me, as Bishop of Scranton, to initiate with the Holy See the complicated but necessary process toward obtaining Basilica status. You can imagine my joy when, four years later, His Eminence returned with the blessing of His Holiness, Pope John Paul the Great, for the solemn dedication of the Basilica of the National Shrine of St. Ann. I consider this one of the special blessings of my years when I was privileged to serve as Bishop of Scranton.

My joy was compounded when I learned that an outstanding Passionist, Fr. Cassian, CP, who has served the Church so well locally and globally, had willingly begun the task of gathering these personal testimonies of the devotees of St. Ann in order to share them with all the faithful. I was very happy to read the manuscript and honored to contribute this preface. I found the brief history of St. Ann's as presented by Fr. Charles P. Connor, Ph.D., historian of our diocese, very fascinating and exciting. I join my voice to that of the Superior General of the Passionists and Fr. Cassian in hoping to see a full-length history of the Basilica, the Novena, the coal mines, and the Passionists' foundation in the famous Round Woods of Scranton.

These excellent testimonies speak for themselves. I found them exciting, moving, and very edifying. I, too, am sure there are hundreds more waiting to be told.

However, I found three truths of our faith of special importance to this book. I believe they contain the substance of what faith and devotion at the Basilica of the National Shrine of St. Ann are all about.

The first of these is indeed the foundation of the entire experience. I refer to the doctrinal basis as described in chapter 5. It is well expressed:

The truth is we belong to two worlds simultaneously and continually: the invisible world of God and the visible world of this creation. In the first and real world, the world without end, the angels and the Saints with the Blessed Virgin Mary and her divine son, Jesus, live in joyful peace by the power of the Holy Spirit to the glory of God the Father. Into the second, the world that will pass away, by the act of God I am created an immortal spirit-soul and joined to my mortal body in the womb of my mother at the moment of conception.

Between these two worlds, the world of man and the world of God, there is continuous, uninterrupted communication, an unending exchange of love and blessing, of grace and favor. It is what the Communion of Saints is all about.

At the great Basilica of St. Ann in Scranton, the exchange between these two worlds — the world of God and the world of man — is made visible, effective, and actual.

The second truth is so dear to all of us. It is a truth preached and experienced at St. Ann's from the very beginning of the Solemn Novena, eighty years ago. It is this: life is sacred from conception to natural death (chapter 9). This great truth of our faith leads to the indispensable role of mother and father in the faith life of their children and the sanctity of marriage (chapters 6 and 7).

Our author measures the importance of these truths in a very practical way, in feet:

> . . . in terms of thousands of feet over these past eighty years and more. The feet of toddlers taking their first steps on these holy grounds. The feet of children running up and down this holy hill from the Grotto to the food stand and back again. The vigorous and agile feet of youth ready to climb to the moon, the tired feet of hard-working parents struggling to make a good life for their children, and the slow but deliberate feet of Grandma and Grandpa who just had to come to say, "Thank you, St. Ann," yet once again.

The third great truth so well put forth in this volume is the power of faith to heal. Chapter 10 is worth reading again and again:

Today, more than ever before, a new understanding of faith has captured our minds. Perhaps it is due to the enormous amount of suffering and evil we have experienced in recent times: the natural disasters like the tsunami in Asia; the terrible hurricanes like Katrina; the devastation of war, especially in Africa, in Iraq, and the Near East; the horrendous and continuous assault upon precious life in the womb; the crushing pandemic of AIDS; the increase in violent crimes, particularly among the young. The new understanding of faith today responds to our urgent need — the need for healing. In every disaster mentioned above, it is faith that brings healing.

In the wild 1960s, faith was mocked — laughed at. It was something for old men and women. It was good for children. Not so today. To be without faith is to be alone and lonely in a confused and disturbing world. It is a sickness.

The healing power of faith is the power of Jesus ever active, ever present.

I am so very happy to see this excellent book made available not only to our people in the immediate vicinity of St. Ann's, but indeed, to the entire Church. And that is what a Basilica is all about: its doors are wide open to the universal Church, to all peoples of every nationality, of every race, clime, and region.

Before closing, I wish to add a personal note — my own testimony. Since the day of my birth until this very day I have lived under the patronage of St. Ann. As a child with my parents, I climbed the holy hill to this Sacred Shrine. I believe my vocation to the priesthood was to a large degree inspired and further developed through my devotion to St. Ann. And as Bishop I continued to participate and to assist at the annual Solemn Novena. I have witnessed the power of faith that this fine book invites all of us to share.

Today's generations will find a greater intensity of faith as they pray in the Basilica. As the future unfolds, this shrine will become internationally acclaimed as pilgrims from many continents travel to Scranton to seek the intercession of St. Ann. May our Saint, mother of Mary, intercede for us always.

MOST REVEREND JAMES C. TIMLIN, D.D.
Bishop Emeritus of Scranton

INTRODUCTION

I OWE MY PASSIONIST VOCATION to my mom and her very dear lifelong friend St. Ann. Mom never told me this until I was ordained. She did not want to interfere with what God was wanting to say to me or to where God might be calling me. But even before I was born, she prayed, "If you give me a boy [in those days they had no way of knowing], please Lord, call him to your side as a priest." When I was a baby she brought me to St. Ann and to the Passionist priests in their long black robes for blessing with the relic of St. Ann.

The first answer to my mom's prayers came when I was in fourth grade. I won first prize in a Bible storytelling contest. I had more stories to tell than any of my thirty classmates. (Each night my father would tell me another story before I went to bed.) When I won first prize my father made me go back with the prize and tell the good Sister, a Sister of St. Cyril and Methodius from Danville, Pennsylvania, that I got all the stories not on my own but from my father. He read the Bible every day after work in the mines. Thank God she allowed me to keep the prize.

The prize was a beautiful crucifix. The good Sister then directed me to hold the crucifix high above the heads of my classmates and then to present the crucifix to each one to venerate by kissing the sacred wounds of Jesus. She gave me a newly pressed handkerchief.

As I went from one classmate to another I was deeply moved by their devotion. That scene never left me; it is with me today.

The second response to my mother's prayer came in my first year of high school. One Monday night after the Novena devotions, I'm standing by my mom, and one of her buddies shook her finger in my mom's face and declared, "Mrs. Yuhas, let me tell you something. If you really want something, say the Stations of the Cross every day. Let me tell you, it never fails."

Well, I sure wanted something. I wanted to know where I was going and how to get there. After the fourth-grade experience, I'm now a freshman in high school — a pretty big kid, as I thought. And I did not know what I should do — what I should be. I began to make the Stations, the Way of the Cross, every day after school — throughout my high school years. I was just a freshman when I began.

When at the end of the stations you finished No. Fourteen, you found yourself face-to-face with a large, life-size crucifix. The sacred wounds were dripping with blood. The deep and sad eyes of Jesus looked right through you. I looked back. What does it mean?

My pastor, a very zealous and rigorous man, Msgr. Joseph Gavenda, knew what it meant. I should enter the seminary. I should join him in Scranton, as a diocesan priest. Certainly! And he prepared my way to enter the prestigious Roman Seminary at Josephenum, in Worthington, Ohio, and from there to Rome. But to his great dismay, a few weeks before departure I reneged. He was not happy, to put it mildly. I had just finished high school. The Monsignor put me on a seven-day retreat with a new book on the priesthood to study every day before and after his daily lecture. I was still waiting for a sign from God.

Then one night at church, St. Joseph's Hazleton, a missionary priest appeared. He wore that long black robe with a badge (the Sign) on his heart: "the Passion of Jesus Christ." He held high the Cross as I did over my classmates. I looked up. I cried. I knew.

I was accepted at Holy Cross Passionist Seminary at Dunkirk, New York, and then I entered the Passionist novitiate at St. Paul of the Cross Monastery in Pittsburgh, Pennsylvania. (Msgr. Gavenda actually drove me to the railroad station.) I made my vows of poverty, perpetual chastity, obedience, and devotion to the Sacred Passion of Jesus in 1944.

Then began that long, long road of theological and scriptural study. Along the way, while preparing my first doctorate in Rome, one little third-grader asked me how long was I going to school. I told him the fact — this was my twenty-fifth consecutive year of study. He looked up at me in wide-eyed amazement and said, "You must be dumb!"

Well, as dumb as I was, I began an even longer road as priest, professor, teacher, writer, lecturer, research director, and preacher, across the country and across the world, filling some eighty-seven volumes of research.

When I was finally assigned to St. Ann's I was delighted to find the great Novena vigorous and alive — every Monday from 7:00 a.m. to 9:00 p.m. and every July from the seventeenth to the twenty-sixth, the glorious feast day.

I received a letter from Chicago. The lady said, "I saw you on TV and had to write." She went on to say, "I owe my life to St. Ann. I was born a cripple. Eventually I was able to walk with crutches with difficulty. Every year my parents brought me to St. Ann's in July. In my thirteenth year I dropped the crutches. You must have them somewhere." She concluded with exuberant thanks, again saying that at a youthful seventy-five, she still scampers up and down "these terrible hills of Chicago."

More wonderful stories came to me. In a research paper on St. Ann's written by our Province historian and archivist, Fr. Robert Carbonneau, CP, I read that even in the early years of the Novena some 3,444 letters and notes of thanks had been received.

I resolved that these marvelous happenings should not go untold. One Monday at all the devotions I made the announcement that I would write the book. I received dozens of responses. A book was born: *Speaking of Miracles: The Faith Experience at the Basilica of the National Shrine of St. Ann.*

I was very happy that my illustrious student Fr. Richard Frechette, CP, priest and doctor, was willing to join me in this work. We decided on two things.

First, after a brief history of the origins of the shrine Basilica and the great Novena, for which we are indebted to Fr. Charles Connor, rector of the Cathedral and historian of the Diocese of Scranton, we would present the doctrinal and scriptural basis for all these miraculous happenings and for the Novena itself.

Second, for the most part, to respect the privacy of contributors, in many cases individuals are not identified in this book. However, all the original and signed letters used in this book are preserved in the monastery archives of St. Ann's Basilica under seal. In case of urgent need, access to these letters may be had only with the permission and supervision of the Father Rector.

We also agreed that we would share with you our understanding of miracles and the miraculous, the Church's understanding and teaching about these spectacular events.

We are a Church of mysteries and miracles. Both have been present in the Church since the birth of Jesus, and both are present today. Mysteries of faith are those divinely revealed truths by which we live: the Divine Trinity; our redemption by the Passion and cruel death of Jesus; the reality of Jesus, Body and Blood, Soul and Divinity in the Eucharist; the beautiful truth of the Blessed and Immaculate Virgin Mary, Mother of God, Mother of the Christ; and so many more profound mysteries of our faith.

Miracles confirm our faith. They occurred almost every day in the public life of Jesus. Jesus was so clear on this. To the doubters, the Scribes, and Pharisees He said, "If you will not believe me on my word, then believe because of the signs (miracles) I perform: the blind see, the deaf hear, the crippled walk and even the dead come back to life."

From the day of Jesus, until this day, miracles and the miraculous have never left the Church. They go hand in hand. Our living faith calls forth the miraculous intervention of God. Miracles confirm the truths of our faith.

Miracles and miraculous interventions are of two kinds. But first we must be clear on what the Church means by a miracle. A miracle is an event or an occurrence for one person or for many persons that has no human explanation. It is an immediate divine intervention.

Miracles for the Church, then, are of two kinds: first, those divine interventions that are thoroughly investigated and examined by the Church using the highest professional skills available. These are subsequently solemnly approved by the Church's highest authority and presented to all the faithful as authentic and worthy of our full belief and acceptance. We see the hand of God.

These miracles may affect large groups of people, even thousands, such as the apparitions of the Blessed Virgin Mary at Lourdes, the "dance of the sun" at Fatima, and the continuous miraculous image of Our Lady of Guadalupe in Mexico, or they may affect one individual person, as the young man I saw who was born blind. His parents from Pittsburgh brought him to St. Ann de Beaupré in Canada every year. In his nineteenth year, he suddenly screamed, "I see! I see!" His sight was given to him in an instant. To this category of instant and complete cures belong all those miracles that are required before a person is beatified (declared Blessed) or canonized (declared a Saint). Each and every one of the miracles have been thoroughly investigated and finally approved by the Church. They number in the thousands. The Church maintains a full-time professional staff in Rome whose only task is to examine the authenticity of reported miracles and present their findings to the Holy Father, who gives the final approval.

All the above pertains to the first category of miracles: those miracles that are solemnly approved by the Church's highest authority.

The second category of miracles is even larger than the first. To the second category of miracles belong all the miraculous occurrences, those divine interventions that happen daily in the Church throughout the world. They have not been taken up by the Church for examination and approval. Their authenticity depends upon the veracity and integrity of the individual reporting the miraculous event and upon eyewitnesses of the event. The individuals know very well what happened to them. The eyewitnesses know. The family knows. The doctor knows. It is this category of miracles and miraculous occurrences that we are privileged to share with you in this book.

What you are receiving is the direct, actual account of a miraculous event in the life of these privileged people. Their urgent prayers have been heard because all of us have joined our prayers to their prayers so that through the intercession of our glorious patron, St. Ann, and of our holy Father and Founder, St. Paul of the Cross, and St. Gabriel, the patron of youth, God will show again His tender love and mercy.

I know these are but a few reports. I am certain there are hundreds more. But these are the first responses I received, and not wanting to delay this long-awaited book, Fr. Richard and I joyfully and gratefully present them to you with our reflections. There may need to be a volume 2 and perhaps even a volume 3 — God knows.

There remains for me the privileged duty of saying, "Thanks. Where to begin?"

In the first place I must thank all of you who so willingly shared with me your experience of faith at the Basilica of St. Ann. I received so many testimonies. Even though I was not able to publish all the letters I received, I am grateful, however, to each and all. Second, I want to thank my rector, Very Rev. Richard Burke, CP, and my community of St. Ann's for their constant encouragement and support. It goes without saying, I am very grateful to my illustrious student and very dear friend Dr. and Fr. Richard Frechette, CP, and to that very dear lifelong friend of St. Ann's Mr. Joseph Connor and his son, the Diocesan historian, Fr. Charles Connor. To these I must add Joseph and Paula Dane and the family of our beloved Ang Ciccotti. Deserving of special tribute are Bill and Eileen Christian, who gave me many insightful improvements and who bore with me through seemingly endless corrections in preparing the manuscript for the publisher. To them I gratefully join Jan Herman and Kathy Porter, extraordinary secretaries. In the same line I wish to say a special thanks to Paul McMahon of Paulist Press who patiently stood by me until the book was born. Finally I must thank my family who not so gently said to me again and again, "For God's sake, in honor of St. Ann, and for peace in the family, GET THE BOOK DONE."

Chapter One

THE PASSIONISTS

H E WAS A VIBRANT nineteen-year-old anxious to find his place in life. His father knew. He should be a merchant and make lots of money and do well. His priest-uncle knew. He should, of course, be a priest. The attractive young lady from one of the "better" families knew. He should marry her.

None of these would work. Paul Francis Danei was destined to become a world leader in another way: by lifting high the Cross.

One day a different Lady came to him. She was so beautiful, and yet so sorrowful. She wore a long black robe with a white heart embossed upon it with a Cross above it, and inside the heart was one word: Jesus.

This is the Lady he would follow to the end of his life. She told him to gather companions and to found a new religious order. They would wear the garment she wore, and they would proclaim to the world the power and the glory, the love and the awesome mystery of Jesus, and Him crucified.

Not long after this great vision, Paul presented himself to the Bishop of Alexandria in North Italy, the Barnabite Bishop, Bishop Albeus di Gattinarra. Paul Danei was vested in the black habit of the Passion. He became Paul of the Cross. The Passionists were born. It was Friday, November 22, 1720, at 4:30 in the afternoon.

For fifty-five years, by day and by night, Paul of the Cross was interviewing candidates, receiving their vows of poverty, chastity, and obedience, and the special vow to the Passion of Jesus, building monasteries and houses of formation for the young, and fulfilling the hopes of the sweet but sorrowful Lady who changed his life forever.

Before dying Paul of the Cross was given a most extraordinary vision: he saw his followers clothed in that same black garment carrying to the entire world the Sign over their hearts, the Cross in their hands, and the name of Jesus on their lips. He was assured his community of the Passion would last until the end of time.

> We are aware that the Passion of Christ continues in this world until He comes in glory; therefore, we share in the joys and sorrows of our contemporaries as we journey through life toward our Father. We wish to share in the distress of all, especially those who are poor and neglected; we seek to offer them comfort and to relieve the burden of their sorrow. (From *The Passionist Rule*)

Paul's vision is being fulfilled each day. Today the Passionist community is truly global. The Passionists are in sixty-three nations. They number over 2,200 followers at the present moment and more than 13,500 since Paul's day.

Today in Africa there are 136 Passionists.

In North America there are 264 Passionists.

In South America there are 452 Passionists.

In Italy and its missions in Bulgaria, Sweden, and the Near East there are 528 Passionists.

In Spain and Portugal there are 235 Passionists.

In England, Ireland, Scotland, and Western Europe there are 289 Passionists.

In Asia (Australia, the Philippines, India, China, Japan, Indonesia, and Korea) there are 318 Passionists.

In the United States, they cover the country from north to south (Boston to North Palm Beach, Florida) and east to west (New York to Los Angeles). Three Passionist priests and one brother arrived in Pittsburgh in November 1852 at the invitation of the first Bishop of Pittsburgh, Most Rev. Michael O'Connor, who became the first and most noteworthy benefactor of the Passionists. The good Bishop provided the land on which they would build their first Monastery dedicated to St. Paul of the Cross, and he sustained them with food, housing, and clothing for their first three years in America. It would take this new community of priests and brothers fifty more years before they discovered Scranton, Pennsylvania.

Wherever they go their mission is one and the same. It is the same for every Passionist priest, brother, cleric, novice, and associate. In very succinct and challenging terms, their mission is *"To preach the Gospel of the Passion by the way they live and by the way they work."*

Every Passionist leads a double life — a hidden life of prayer and personal penance observing the perpetual vows of poverty, chastity, and obedience, and a public life of work and apostolic zeal.

It is hoped that these lives will blend into one single expression of holiness of life in the imitation of Jesus, and Him crucified. This imitation is nowhere better expressed than in the love for others, the famous "neighbor" of the Gospels.

That is why the greatest boast of the Passionists and their greatest joy is in those who have succeeded well in doing this. They are Passionist heroes. They beckon us to follow in their footsteps. Many of them you know well. We want you to know them all.

You know St. Paul of the Cross himself, Father and Founder; you know St. Gabriel, patron of youth; St. Gemma Galgani; and there are so many others — to name a few more: St. Vincent, Blessed Dominic Barberi, Blessed Fr. Charles.

Altogether there are five Passionist canonized Saints, thirty-six Passionists beatified (one step from canonization), sixteen who have been declared heroic or venerable (being prepared for beatification), fourteen other Servants of God (whose cause has begun). Besides all these there are eleven more who are recognized for outstanding holiness of life. Among them we are proud to note three Americans: the famous convert and college president (two colleges actually) Fr. Fidelis Kent Stone, CP; the Passionist from Springfield, Massachusetts, and former teacher of many of us and General Superior of all of us, Fr. Theodore Foley; and the gifted missionary Fr. Henry Vetter, CP.

To these we wish to add yet another: the Passionist best known among us as the father and founder of the great Novena to St. Ann, the friend of the poor, the sick, the forgotten, and the little people: Fr. John Joseph Endler, CP.

The most important thing about the Passionists is not what they do but how they live and love in the shadow of the Cross of Jesus crucified.

Chapter Two

DISCOVERING SCRANTON, PENNSYLVANIA

A N EARLY CHRONICLER writing about the Passionists in Scranton in 1907 made this very relevant point:

> It is always interesting to go back to the beginnings of a great work, and always the more interesting to find those beginnings laid in humility and obscurity, and containing little promise. And then, to look at that work as we have it today — a record of achievement and combined success.[1]

This story of achievement and success had its beginnings in a rather unlikely place — St. Francis Rectory in Nanticoke, Pennsylvania. The pastor there in December 1900 was Fr. James Martin. He had invited the Passionist Fathers to give a mission in his parish, and two of them came in the persons of Frs. Gabriel Fromm and Benedict Manley. In the course of their visit, Fr. Martin mentioned to them a beautiful spot he was familiar with on the Susquehanna River just opposite Nanticoke. He felt it would be a perfect spot for a Passionist retreat and asked the Fathers to consider it. Also, during the same parish mission, the pastor invited Bishop Michael J. Hoban, second Bishop of the diocese, to come down and meet with the Passionist priests.

This chapter was written by the Very Reverend Charles P. Connor, Ph.D., rector of the Cathedral and historian of the Diocese of Scranton.

Bishop Hoban was by no means a stranger to the Passionists. He was a native of New Jersey who grew up in Pennsylvania's Wayne County community of Hawley and studied at the North American College in Rome in preparation for his ordination to the priesthood for the Diocese of Scranton. While in Rome, he had often visited the Passionist Generalate on the Coelian Hill, the famous Basilica of Sts. John and Paul, built over the home of two brothers, martyrs of the early Church. He made his ordination retreat there, said his first Mass at the tomb of Peter in the Vatican, and the following day said his second Mass at the tomb of St. Paul of the Cross, the Passionist Founder, whose remains are to be found in a side chapel in this wonderful Roman church which, since the time of Francis Cardinal Spellman, has been the titular church of the Cardinal Archbishops of New York. At this second Mass, the young Fr. Hoban was assisted by Fr. Fidelis, who in his earlier life had been known as Dr. James Kent Stone, president of two colleges: Kenyon College in Gambier, Ohio, and Hobart in Geneva, New York.

Early in 1900, some months before the Nanticoke mission, Bishop Hoban had traveled to Rome in company with two Passionist friends, Frs. Luke Baudinelli and Felix Ward, and he found his old friend Fidelis Kent Stone now a general consultor at Sts. John and Paul. Hoban told the Passionists in Nanticoke that evening that on the Rome visit Pope Leo XIII had told him it would be an opportune time in the history of his diocese to introduce a religious community of men. Communication began at once with the superior general of the Passionists to set the process in motion.

The first site that Fr. Martin suggested was not as workable as at first thought, and several other locales were examined. The difficulty the Fathers faced was that Northeastern Pennsylvania was an area of hard coal mines — one of the major industries which built the region — and there was always the very real fear of mine subsidence. So they had to be careful which site they selected; little did they know what was in store at the site they finally chose. Initially, the Lacoe cottage at Harvey's Lake was chosen as a residence, and Fr. Fidelis Kent Stone became the first superior. He was accompanied by Frs. Gregory and Eugene, and they took up residence on May 11, 1902. Two rooms on the first floor were turned into a chapel, and the local residents (mostly summer dwellers) began attending daily Mass. Almost immediately, Fr. Fidelis began looking for a permanent site.

The general chapter of the Passionists in August 1902 was the meeting at which a permanent site for a monastery was discussed, and by the time the chapter met, the Round Woods, an area southwest of central Scranton, was the leading "contender." The Passionists had some very real fears for their safety, building here, once again because of the mine situation. Bishop Hoban assured them such fears were unwarranted. He had secured a diagram of the mines, with written affidavits by competent engineers attesting to the area's safety, and with such assurance, plans went ahead for building a monastery.

It was on September 8, 1902, that the final decision was made, and shortly thereafter construction began — but to whom should the monastery be dedicated? There were some in the community who felt it should bear the name of St. Andrew — "the Apostle of the Cross and Passion" as he is sometimes called. But since these conversations took place on the feast of the Nativity of the Blessed Virgin Mary, one of the consultors to the Passionist provincial suggested our Lady's mother, St. Ann. He is supposed to have made the comment, "St. Ann will take care of her own," and St. Ann was already recognized as the Patron Saint of Miners. Ten acres were purchased, and they were described as "forming a plateau rather high above the city." The description continues, "It slopes gently on all sides and commands a splendid view of the city and surrounding hills and valleys. At one time it was covered by a dense wood and mountain growth, affording shade in the sultry summer and a resort for family picnics."

The fathers rented a home on Sloan Street near South Main, moved in on October 22, 1902, and were saying the public Masses by All Souls' Day. The first church of St. Ann was blessed on Christmas Eve, 1902, at the corner of Sloan and South Main streets on the land given them by Mr. Patrick Mulhern. The original five-story monastery is remembered well. It was begun the following year, 1903, with Owen McGlynn of Wilkes-Barre the architect. The cornerstone was laid in September of that year amid great fanfare, and Fr. Thomas Comerford of Archbald preached the sermon. Bishop Hoban's remarks on that occasion were almost prophetic:

> France drove the religious orders out. Scranton welcomed them in. France had nothing to fear but their prayers and work for souls, and this is just what Scranton wants, the prayers and works of the Passionist Fathers for the souls of our people. Their record here will be one of untold usefulness and blessings to us. They are welcome to Scranton. In your name and my own I bid them a thousand welcomes and I ask God's blessings for all who will aid them in the building of their home on this hill. Again with all my heart I bid them welcome to the Diocese of Scranton.... [2]

Mass was offered in the monastery chapel for the first time on the feast of the Annunciation, March 25, and the solemn dedication of the monastery took place the following July in the presence of the Apostolic Delegate to the United States. Fr. Albert Phelan was elected first canonical rector, and a Passionist historian, recounting one of the earliest events of significance in the new monastery, records this:

On June 30, 1906, nine of our Passionist students and ten seminarians of the diocese were ordained priests at the Cathedral by Bishop Hoban. All made the retreat in preparation at St. Ann's. The exercises were conducted by Fr. Aloysius Blakely, CP, of happy memory. Since that date the Bishop has sent the seminarians to the Retreat to prepare for ordination, and a bond of affection between these good priests and the Passionists has been one of the results.[3]

Even earlier than this, 1903, land had been purchased by two different priests across "St. Ann's Boulevard" for the building of a school and convent. The school building would initially house them and the hall and parish house. The Sisters, Servants of the Immaculate Heart of Mary from Marywood promised to staff the parish school.

On the feast of St. Ann, July 26, 1908, Bishop Hoban dedicated the new church and hall. Fr. Fidelis Kent Stone sang the Mass of Dedication.

The Passionists continued to prosper, developing the entire area of the Round Woods. They attracted more and more people; they conducted retreats at the monastery and missions and "Forty Hours" not only in the Scranton Diocese but in neighboring dioceses as well. And the anthracite mining industry likewise continued to expand and flourish, drawing increased numbers of young families to the area. But despite the good reports, disaster was about to strike not once, but twice with greater severity and danger.

The Rock Foundation:
From Near Ending to a Fresh Beginning

On the feast of the Assumption of the Blessed Virgin Mary, August 15, 1911, a crisis of monumental proportions occurred:

a very serious disturbance underneath the property caused by subsidence in the coal mines significantly injured the entire structure. Most of the Passionist community were sent to other monasteries, while a skeleton crew remained to look after the spiritual needs of the people here at St. Ann's.

Eventually the situation seemed safe. Engineers reported that the subsidence was over, and the work of repairing and strengthening the monastery began. It all seemed to be going very well until July 28, 1913, when disaster struck again. The worst "squeeze" known in local mining occurred. The priests were told it was not safe for anyone to remain in the building; a great slide was carrying the entire Round Woods in an easterly direction, and nothing whatsoever could be done to save the monastery. What was it, then, that accounted for the fact that the mighty slide that threatened to swallow up the monastery and the entire hill stopped, turned back, and settled solidly under the foundations of the monastery? It seemed to reecho an earlier observation that St. Ann would take care of her own.

The engineers and mining inspectors themselves considered the event miraculous. On the fatal day when everyone was ordered off the hill and out of the monastery, the skeleton community determined to remain and redouble the urgency of their prayers to good St. Ann. The following morning, they requested the engineers and inspectors to check yet one more time. They descended. When they emerged, they were astonished beyond words. The unbelievable happened. Three huge boulders — boulders they had never seen before in the weeks of inspection — had locked themselves in an immovable position directly below the monastery: from death to life, from near total collapse to a fresh beginning!

It was well over a year after these events that the Passionist Fathers returned to St. Ann's. Nothing had really been done to prepare the building for the return of the community, until a committee of Catholic laymen took it upon themselves to approach one of the Fathers still in Scranton, Fr. Timothy, and ask if they might be of help. With the approval of Bishop Hoban, the men called a much larger meeting of the local citizenry — hundreds were present, we are told, and they pledged themselves to be part of a large-scale effort to raise money for the necessary repairs to make the building once again livable. A campaign was organized, and the parishes of the diocese were asked to give a helping hand. The outpouring was magnificent, but the amount of money raised fell far short of what was needed. Perhaps more than any group, the temperance society the Knights of Father Matthew raised the needed funds. A great demonstration, a fair was held on the grounds of St. Ann's, sponsored by the Father Matthew men in conjunction with their October parade held each year in the diocese on the anniversary of Father Matthew's birth. The success of this fair closed the campaign, and the rest is part of the history of this holy hill. The monastery was re-dedicated in public ceremonies on July 22, 1915. The Nuncio came from Stroudsburg to Scranton on July 21 in a private car of the president of the Delaware, Lackawanna and Western Railroad. The monastery chronicler gives us a moving account of the event:

On that bright morning of July 22, the people began to assemble on the monastery lawns. The breezes were aromatic and the broad expanse of blue above suggested some heavenly cathedral arranged in dazzling beauty. To the east of the handsome building a great canopy in delicate colors had been arranged with exquisite taste and under it the altar and throne had been erected for Mass in the open air. The procession moved from the north entrance around to the canopy in imposing order and sanctuary vesture; acolytes, scholastics, priests, prelates, bishops, and lastly the papal delegate in pontifical robes, with mitre and crosier, surrounded by his attendants for Mass, with the uniformed Knights of Columbus as a guard of honor. All took their places, the bishops with their chaplains, the prelates next according to rank, then a hundred priests to the left of the altar and fifty sisters of the Immaculate Heart of Mary to their left.... There were twenty thousand people gathered around as the papal delegate in pontifical vesture stood at the foot of the altar with his attendants to begin Mass. The reporters said fifty thousand were assembled.[4]

Years later, in 1926, a letter from Passionist Provincial Fr. Stanislaus Grennan to the Passionist Fr. Benedict Huck, rector of St. Ann's Monastery, clearly shows that a regular weekly St. Ann Novena had emerged as part of a postresurrection experience of the monastery:

We are simply in the same predicament as all Scranton people, and must depend upon the good Lord and the intercession of St. Ann to protect us. Considering the precarious condition of our plant (monastery, church and school) for all times to come, there ought to be a special prayer said daily by the Community to St. Ann to protect her buildings. The recitation of such prayer would be a reminder of our dependence upon her intercession and will evoke many other prayers for the same end.

The great Solemn Novena before the feast of St. Ann, July 26, had begun two years previously, attracting people from all over the United States to join the Passionist community in thanking God and praising good St. Ann, who indeed takes care of her own.

Chapter Three

THE GREAT NOVENA

~~~•~~~

F ROM THE FOUNDATION of the monastery in 1902, devotions to St. Ann were limited primarily to the prayers of the monastic community. Public devotions in the monastery chapel did not begin until November 3, 1924. Years earlier, Fr. Nicholas Ward, CP, an early rector who had exceptional devotion to St. Ann, predicted that the monastery would become a place of very conspicuous testimonials. He did not live to see it, of course, but Fr. Benedict Huck, CP, rector in 1924, implemented that early vision after he noticed a marked increase in the people's devotion to St. Ann. One year later, in 1925, a young priest would arrive at St. Ann's whose dedication to the Novena would become legendary in the Lackawanna Valley.

Fr. John Joseph Endler, CP, was born in Union City, New Jersey, in 1892. He was one of four religious vocations in his family, three to the Passionists and a sister to the Sisters of Charity in Newark. He had been professed in the Passionist congregation in 1913 and ordained ten years later in Boston by William Cardinal O'Connell. For seven years of his life in Scranton he worked tirelessly to spread devotion to St. Ann. He began the Novena in a tent that would be erected each Monday, and he became known for his preaching, his hours in the confessional, and his competent spiritual direction. Priests, religious, and laity all came to him, and none were disappointed. During the Novena's first year, 3,444 letters of thanksgiving for favors granted were received. With the erection of the splendid new church of St. Ann later in the 1920s, devotions were conducted in a more spacious and devotional atmosphere. Fr. John Joseph would go on to serve his community as rector in monasteries in Springfield, Massachusetts, and Dunkirk, New York, and later he went to the Passionist mission in Washington, North Carolina, for work with Southern Catholics. In this assignment he worked closely with the Immaculate Heart of Mary Sisters from Scranton, who staffed the school. He made friends all over the country through the years. Many of these friends were his financial contributors at Mother of Mercy mission. He died in 1957 after a long, lingering illness that brought him intense suffering. For several years his burial place was St. Michael's Monastery in his native Union City, but when that house closed some years ago, and those buried there were exhumed and reburied in a diocesan cemetery, Fr. John Joseph's mortal remains were brought to St. Ann's largely through the efforts of Fr. Berard Tierney, CP. He was solemnly interred in the place of honor in the monastery cemetery of St. Ann beneath the beautiful crucifix. This place overlooks the final resting place of all the Passionist priests and brothers who served St. Ann's before and after the illustrious holy Servant of God Fr. John Joseph Endler, CP, whose cause for canonization has been the hope of thousands of his followers. It is true that no Passionist had a greater impact on the Solemn Novena, no Passionist so energized and revitalized the annual Novena by reason of his charismatic character, his holiness of life, and his dynamic preaching. These qualities led people to venerate him as a Saint and to look upon him as the founder of the Novena, a title he would never claim. The truth is there is not one, but many founders.

The true founders of the Solemn Novena are the people — the devout laity who came first in the hundreds and then in the thousands to join the first community of Passionists, even before the mine disaster, in invoking St. Ann as their special patron. It was, above all, the faith and devotion of the people, a devotion that never diminished, that convinced the authorities in Rome that St. Ann's was indeed worthy of being elevated to the rank of a Basilica for the universal Church.

Obviously, it is not our intention to write the history of St. Ann's Novena. That story is waiting to be written. As our former Superior General, Most Rev. Jose Agustin Orbegozo, CP, noted in a letter to the community on June 29, 2000, on the occasion of the dedication and blessing of the new monastery:

It is a sign of God's favor and blessing upon the great work that all of you together with a large number of devoted laity have accomplished over the many years since a few Passionists carrying the Crucifix, a relic of St. Paul of the Cross, and the relic of St. Ann arrived in the Round Woods of Scranton, Pennsylvania.

The full story of the countless favors and blessings and miracles has yet to be told, but this day and this moment mark a turning point of great significance in the history of St. Ann's of Scranton as you bless and dedicate your new Monastery and Spiritual Center.

We Passionists have been blest by God to proclaim the Gospel of the Passion in several world-famous sanctuaries and shrines. St. Gabriel of Gran Sasso comes to mind at once where several million people journey in pilgrimage each year. We also recall St. Gemma's in Madrid, Our Lady of Help in Austria, the great sanctuary of the Passion in Mexico, St. Ann's in Sutton, England, and the famous Mt. Argus in Ireland.

To these we now proudly add the Basilica of the National Shrine of St. Ann in Scranton, Pennsylvania. May your work continue to flourish bringing hope and peace, healing and solace to the thousands of faithful who turn to St. Ann daily.

I am especially impressed by the number of vocations we have received through this center of faith and devotion. I urge you and all the faithful to intensify your prayers and your programs to increase vocations to our Congregation at a time when requests for the Passionist ministry are so many and so urgent.

To celebrate the centennial of the Passionists in the Diocese of Scranton, St. Ann's Monastery sponsored a lecture series. Fr. Charles Connor, Ph.D., historian of the Diocese of Scranton, gave the first talk: "How It All Began — The Very Beginnings of Passionist Life and Mission in Scranton in 1902." It concentrated on the origins of the great Novena to St. Ann and Fr. John Joseph Endler, CP. This was followed by Fr. Robert Carbonneau, CP, Historian and Director of the Passionist Historical Archives. The subject of his talk was: "How It Grew — Development and Expansion of the Mission and Ministry of St. Ann's from Fr. John Joseph until Modern Times." Finally I gave the concluding talk, "Where We Are Today — Continual Flow of Blessing and Graces at St. Ann's."

This in turn led to the video *The Amazing Story 1902–2002*, produced by Catholic Television, Diocese of Scranton. It consists of an adaptation of the three thirty-minute talks by the centennial speakers. The ninety-minute video can be obtained at the St. Ann's Monastery. Overall, the video can be used as an important tool to foster a historical perspective on the Passionist presence.

These were preliminary studies on the origin and development of the Solemn Novena. However, the most authoritative study to date, which the author claims is still but a beginning of a full history, is the paper by the historian of the Province of St. Paul of the Cross, Fr. Robert Carbonneau, CP, delivered at the University of Scranton on March 29, 2003, for the American Catholic Historical Association. This excellent study subsequently was published in the periodical *American Catholic Studies* 115, no. 2, under the title, "Coal Mines, St. Ann's Novena, and Passionist Spirituality in Scranton, Pennsylvania, 1902–2002." Fr. Carbonneau believes that for a true understanding of the extraordinary phenomena occurring at St. Ann's and to understand the Solemn Novena itself, one needs to place it in a threefold perspective: the anthracite coal mining industry of that time, the evolution and development of a Novena culture, and the establishment of the contemplative community of Passionist nuns in Scranton in 1926.

As the significance and meaning of St. Ann's Basilica continues to reach more and more people, we look forward to the day when we shall have not only an authoritative history of the Solemn Novena, but indeed the history of the entire St. Ann Foundation.

Role of the Media

When that history comes to be written, special attention will be given to the role of the media in promoting and expanding the influence of St. Ann's Basilica.

As far back as 1939 a radio broadcast was made of the St. Ann's Solemn Novena. The first Catholic television program in Scranton was in 1953. This was the *St. Ann Choristers*, a children's choir directed by Fr. Norbert Herman, CP, of St. Ann's Monastery. On February 13, 1955, Fr. Norbert initiated the first televised Mass program in Scranton.

Over the years, the Passionist Fathers of St. Ann's have presented radio programs on various local stations, and Fr. Cyril Schweinberg initiated a TV talk show.

What started as monthly televised broadcasts on the first Sunday of each month back in 1955 soon became weekly telecasts, and for thirty years they remained the only regular local Catholic TV presentation.

On October 6, 1991, the Sunday TV Mass made its debut on a national satellite network. From November 1991 to November 1994 the Catholic Telecommunications Network of America (CTNA) also televised *The Celebration of the Mass.*

May 9, 1993, marked the date for the first telecast of *St. Ann's Weekly Novena,* with Bishop James C. Timlin leading the service. *The Mass* from St. Ann's Basilica is now a national program.

On April 7, 1996, St. Ann's Media launched two sites on the World Wide Web. One site, *www.theMass.org,* provides texts and photos pertaining to the Basilica and to St. Ann's Novena. The other site, *www.prayerline.org,* is an interfaith prayer site. A third site, *www.theMass.com,* features streaming video, including the sacrifice of the Mass, seven days a week, twenty-four hours a day. The value of the Basilica telecasts and the impact they have upon countless people across the nation and beyond is testified to by the flood of mail and the telephone messages that are received daily in the media offices.

Beloved by All

Any account of the Basilica and the Novena that failed to recognize one of the most important leaders would be terribly deficient. After the heroic figure of Fr. John Joseph Endler, no other person did as much to restore the Basilica, build a new monastery, and increase true devotion to St. Ann and the Passionist Saints than Fr. Berard Tierney, CP. Fr. Berard was born and raised in the shadow of the monastery. He took his vows on August 15, 1941, and was ordained a Passionist priest on February 25, 1948. He was born to his eternal life June 15, 2005.

The rector of St. Ann's, Fr. Richard Burke, CP, who worked so closely with him, gave this beautiful summary of his life:

> Our ten days of prayer, devotion and reflection have a wonderful history going back to the ten days between the Ascension of Our Lord and the Gift of the Holy Spirit on us at Pentecost. Here at St. Ann's, our heritage reaches back to Fr. John Joseph Endler, CP, in 1925 when he preached the first Annual Solemn Novena. This year, we are especially mindful of one of our own native sons, Fr. Berard Tierney, CP, whose history with the Novena reaches back to the very first Novena with Fr. John Joseph. We count Fr. Berard among the pioneers of this graced time who lived each day of his life with St. Ann as companion and inspiration. Fr. Berard was a devoted believer in St. Ann's intercessory powers and a dedicated priest for God's people here at St. Ann's, especially over the last thirty-one years. Over these years, Fr. Berard dedicated his time and his energy to preaching at St. Ann's, in various retreat centers and in parishes within and outside our Scranton Diocese. He was a foundational person in the fundraising effort to renovate our beautiful Basilica. Having witnessed the demolition of the original St. Ann's Monastery, he continued to raise funds to build our new St. Ann's Passionist Monastery. Happily, he lived to see its completion and was able to enjoy the final five years of his life in a new home for which he dreamed so often. He counted himself very blessed through the intercession of St. Ann.

Just before we went to press with this book, which Fr. Berard so much wanted to see, a friend of his sent me this spontaneous tribute. He expresses well what thousands of people whose lives have been touched by Fr. Berard would want to say:

Dear Father,

I am writing in tribute to Fr. Tierney and the St. Ann's Monastery.

Having grown up in an environment of very modest means, I continually reflect on what influenced my life, direction and motivation.

I have vivid memories of the yearly Novenas at St. Ann's with the massive turnouts they precipitated and the tradition they created in our family life. We attended every year with relatives from New Jersey who made it nothing less than a pilgrimage.

Without fail for nearly fifty years, my mother would light a candle in the basement chapel every Monday night.

During all this time, I recall Fr. Tierney who it seemed was always serving Mass but would routinely visit our family during sick times, unfortunate events, and all major holidays. I never understood how he found the time to be so very dedicated to the church and to so many people.

I feel very fortunate to have achieved a high level of success in my career and personal life. I could not have done this without the work ethic, family values, integrity, and character that developed through my formative years instilled by my parents, the Boy Scouts, and Fr. Tierney. You don't realize what impacts your life until you look back and evaluate what the building blocks and foundation were to your own success.

Upon reflection, I would say that Fr. Tierney was one of my role models for life, always a positive influence, always even-tempered, always supportive. He was a guiding light that gave us hope during vast periods of hardship in everyday life in Northeastern Pennsylvania.

It is with these very fond and respectful memories that I commemorate his passing.

Chapter Four

REVITALIZATION

A S EARLY AS 1974 on the occasion of the fiftieth anniversary of the Solemn Novena, it was realized that major renovations would be needed both for the monastery and for the church. The monastery was, at that time, more critical than the church. Despite enduring two mine subsidences which left serious cracks in the walls, the monastery served the Passionists and the Diocese of Scranton very well for more than eighty years. Practically every priest ordained for the diocese made his ordination retreat at St. Ann's. By the late 1980s it became painfully evident that monumental changes would need to be made to bring the old, classical, five-story building up to code and render it safe for the enlarged community and a new class of Passionist seminarians. Consultation with several architects and engineers produced a major program of total renovation. However, with it came major cost estimates. An estimate was presented that was prohibitive and far beyond the budget sustainable by the community, and indeed, the Province. After further discussion and new proposals, the Provincial Superior in consultation with the community decided the building had to go.

Of that elegant five-story edifice, only a small area could be salvaged: the old chapel, the former library, meeting rooms, and the front parlor.

It was a sad day for the diocese, for the priests and people, and doubly sad for the community of Passionists. St. Ann's could no longer maintain a class of seminarians, having neither space nor money. The community, reduced in size, had to move down the hill and across the street into the convent once occupied by the Immaculate Heart of Mary Sisters, who for decades had taught in St. Ann's Grammar and High School.

The remnant of the old monastery became the Shrine Center with a receptionist desk, a small gift shop, and a cafeteria that also served for meetings and small parish programs. The priests and brothers commuted daily from the bottom of the hill to the shrine and without interruption continued their service to priests and sisters and people. St. Ann's Parish likewise never interrupted its pastoral care of the parishioners, both in the school and in the church. The parish renovated an old house to serve as rectory, with the parish office and living quarters for the pastor and his associates.

Full attention could now be given to caring for the ailing St. Ann's Church. By 1990 the need for urgent restoration was imperative. In the following year, the rector, Very Rev. Richard Burke, CP, launched a major revitalization campaign entitled "Of Faith and Devotion" with an immediate goal of $3 million and a long-range goal of $6 million. A Revitalization Committee was formed under the leadership of Msgr. Andrew McGowan, Joe and Paula Dane, Ang Ciccotti, and Joseph Connor, with Fr. Berard Tierney, CP, as chairperson and guide. The other members were Paul Byrne, William Byrne Sr., William F. Calpin, Barbara A. Cawley, Nancy Cawley, Joseph Cianci, James Clauss, Mary Ellen Coleman, Joseph N. Connor, Joesph Corcoran, Thomas Cummings, William P. Cusick, Louis DeNaples, John Dieta, Christopher DiMattio, Gary Drapek, Gerard Ferrario, Tim E. Foley, Mary Ellen Gizzi, Gerald T. Griffin, David Hemmler, Leo P. Higgins, Nancy Kay Holmes, Robert T. Kelly Jr., Arthur Kenney, David Lencicki, Pat Loughney, Edward J. and Linda Lynett, Claire Maldonato, Dominick J.

Maldonato, Patrick J. Manley, John R. McCabe, John E. McDonald, Marge McGee, Joseph Munley, Rose Ann Murphy, Dom Netti, Barbara Noto, Judy O'Malley, Mary Gardier Paterson, George and Barbara Pegula, Joseph Quinn, Dominick Scartelli, Carolyn Shegelski, Gerard Smith, Tim Speicher, David Tressler, Ann Williams, and Andrew Yaniga.

The committee was energized when it learned of the possibility of St. Ann's being elevated to the dignity and honor of a Basilica. This hope was confirmed when His Eminence, Achille Cardinal Silvestrini, Secretary of the Council for the Public Affairs of the Church under Pope John Paul II, visited St. Ann's on October 26, 1993. His Eminence offered a special liturgy that evening with a full church attendance. At the reception that followed in the school hall, the Cardinal stood from 9:00 p.m. until midnight listening as each one stood in line to tell the Cardinal what St. Ann's meant to each person. Afterward before sitting down to a midnight *pranzo*, His Eminence told the community he believed from all he heard that St. Ann's was, indeed, worthy to be named a Basilica and he, himself, would intercede for us. Thus began a long period of trial, interrogation, and investigation to determine whether or not St. Ann's would qualify for the honor. The process begins with the local Bishop. He, himself, must be convinced and on his own initiative make the request of the Holy Father, for only the Pope has the authority to name a Basilica.

Bishop Timlin's testimony was loud and clear. From his childhood, in his mother's arms, he had learned true devotion to St. Ann, a devotion that increased year after year throughout his priesthood and episcopal consecration. The Bishop's petition went first to the Conference of Bishops of the U.S.A. The Conference has a special committee on shrines and pilgrimages.

The episcopal committee then makes its own independent investigation. Its conclusion, which was so favorable to St. Ann's is, in turn, presented to the full Conference. The Bishops of the United States, then, forwarded their petition with their approval to the Holy Father. You would think that the trial would end with so prestigious a request. But it does not. Rome, itself, must make its own investigation with its own team and its own principles and criteria. At this point, everyone asks why this is so complicated. What is a Basilica?

A Basilica is not an empty name. It is not an honorary title. *It is a fact: a fact of profound faith.*

What makes a Basilica is the factual witness of tens of thousands of people over many generations testifying to the sacredness of a Shrine: that a certain place is indeed a place of God's special blessing, of God's favor and grace.

St. Ann's is just such a place. Countless are the blessings and favors granted to thousands upon thousands of people from all over this land and beyond, people of all ages: infants in arms, youth, married couples, families, the aged and infirm. They come in a continuous line stretching back over ten decades to offer their prayers and petition to good St. Ann, grandmother of us all.

There is a truth to the saying "Basilicas are made in heaven, not on earth." The Basilica is, indeed, a gift of God.

By designating a holy shrine as a Basilica the Church is but acknowledging the fact of extraordinary faith and genuine devotion manifest at the Shrine. Everyone is welcomed at a Basilica.

At St. Ann's National Shrine, that faith and devotion is increasing year after year, and it is destined to continue.

With the Basilica status, St. Ann's is raised to a new position in the Church. It is no longer simply another church maintained and served by the Passionist community. It is more than a parish within the Diocese of Scranton. It belongs to the universal Church. It is given global recognition and value.

In a special way, it pertains to the Holy See and the Pope, for it is the Holy Father who alone has the authority to elevate a Shrine to the status of Basilica. It is for this reason that the first in order of priority and the most distinctive mark of a Basilica is the presentation and use of the papal coat of arms internally and externally, on literature, correspondence, and so forth.

Basilicas are intended to be not only centers of particular and more intense devotion and prayer, but traditionally Basilicas have been centers for study and research, for education and Christian formation, for promoting a deeper understanding and a more active participation in the major goals and objectives of the universal Church. The Church has a right to turn to the Basilica and expect more from it.

Finally, after further study, all these investigations went favorably for St. Ann's, and on August 29, 1996, Pope John Paul II issued the papal decree elevating St. Ann's Shrine to the honor and the dignity of a Minor Basilica with all the rights and privileges that attach to it. (Minor because there are only four Major Basilicas, all in Rome: St. Peter's, St. Paul's, St. Mary Major, and St. John Lateran.)

Our dear friend Cardinal Silvestrini returned to Scranton one year later, on October 18, 1997, and in the name of the Pope, John Paul II, dedicated the National Shrine of St. Ann a Basilica. It was a great day! Special gifts were presented to the Shrine on that night: the papal bell and the papal umbrellino. They are to remain in the Basilica as a permanent reminder of the Pope's blessing and the day of dedication. They have a charming history. In medieval times only the Pope in person could dedicate a Basilica. An acolyte walked before him ringing a big bell to announce the arrival of the Pope. So no one would lose sight of him, a large, colorful umbrella was carried above him. When the Pope left he said, "I leave you my umbrella and my bell as a perpetual remembrance of my presence and my blessings."

During the entire time while the preparations were being completed for the Basilica, members of the Revitalization Committee repeatedly said to the Passionist Fathers, "What about yourselves? You have no suitable place to live. You need a home." Indeed, they did. They gave proof to an old saying among the clergy, "In the Catholic Church there is no appointment more permanent than a temporary assignment." When the community had to move down the hill and across the street, it was to be but temporary, a few years or so. That already dilapidated and incommodious building became their home for twenty years.

Members of the Revitalization Committee with the Basilica Community of St. Ann's immediately gave their attention to a new campaign. A "Coming Home" campaign was started to raise the money needed to build a new monastery. In the July 1999 issue of the Novena newsletter, this joyful moment was expressed in these words:

Coming Home

People cried as they watched the old monastery being demolished. The priests and brothers had to move out. For twenty years they had been living in a so-called temporary residence. During these long years the cry of the people was constant: "Come home," "Come back up the hill," "Come to where you belong."

But they could not move. The Passionist priests and brothers had neither the money nor the time nor the energy. All their time and all their money had to be given to rescuing the beautiful but endangered church of St. Ann. That effort took several years, in which time they raised over three million dollars. The Passionists and their excellent group of laymen and women were all greatly encouraged. They were inspired to work even harder when word was received from Rome that the Holy Father, Pope John Paul II, was considering the possibility of raising St. Ann's to the status and dignity of a Basilica.

Meanwhile the priests and brothers, while devoting themselves completely to the Basilica project, continued for twenty years, day after day and in all kinds of weather, to scramble across the street and up to the Basilica and back down to their dilapidated "temporary" residence.

And then the dream came true. At last the foundation is in. The Passionists are building. On the ruins of the ancient monastery, a new one is rising! A Passionist monastery is much more than a mere residence, a place to hang up your hat and grab a cup of soup. It is a center of prayer and spirituality. It is a refuge for countless numbers of people, young and old and in between, who seek help in their many needs. It is a center of study and preparation for ministry. It is a welcoming hearth to shelter and nourish lonely, depressed and saddened people. It is a missionary center sending priests and brothers to all parts of these United States and beyond.

Come spring 2000 and the priests and brothers will move in! The timing is right. The Passionists achieved the status of Basilica granted by Pope John Paul II, a very distinct honor. This year marks the 75th anniversary of the great Novena to St. Ann and the Passionist Saints.

It is an amazing fact to know that not only thousands but actually millions of people have been helped through this great devotion. Countless are the favors and blessings received throughout these seventy-five years — healings for mind, for the body and soul, marriages repaired, families reunited, properties sold, jobs obtained, successful surgeries, the gift of new life to the formerly childless couples — the list goes on and on.

The timing is right. The Passionists will begin the new millennium from their new monastery residence atop the hill, next to the great Basilica. They are coming home!

The Revitalization Program had two principal goals: to complete, renovate, refurbish and beautify the Shrine Church of St. Ann so as to make it worthy of the special blessing conferred upon it by Our Holy Father, Pope John Paul II, and secondly, to build a new home for the Basilica Community. With the generous and willing cooperation of so many devoted clients of St. Ann, these two goals have been well achieved. There was yet a third goal to be achieved: the Holy Grounds of St. Ann's.

The revitalization of these Holy Grounds began with the Stations of the Cross, always a center of devotion for the thousands of clients of St. Ann, year after year. The Stations were completely renewed and made very accessible to our people. But of special note was the building of a memorial walk from Station One to Station Fourteen. The memorial walk consists of bricks, marble and granite blocks on which are inscribed the names of donors, benefactors, friends and family, living or deceased, who will be remembered each time we pray the Stations of the Cross. This program has been very successful as each year pilgrims come from all over our country to see their name and the names of their loved ones inscribed in the Memorial Walk. Special tribute is due to Mr. Joseph Dane and his wife, Paula, who first proposed this excellent project and have continued to promote it ever since.

Together with the renewal of the Way of the Cross, four grottos have been developed, two old and two new.

The old ones are well known but had been neglected over the years. They are the Grotto of Gethsemane and the Grotto of St. Gemma. Gethsemane, the Agony in the

Garden, has been especially loved by our people. It is now available to all with a beautiful plaza of marble and granite blocks. St. Gemma Grotto has also been restored.

Two new grottos have been developed, the first to St. Joseph the Worker. This grotto is dedicated to all the lay volunteers who have been with us throughout these years of revitalization — some of them for more than ten years!

The second new grotto is to Our Lady of the Angels and is set in the middle of a rose garden and just below the beautiful cemetery where the Passionist priests and brothers who served at St. Ann's from the earliest years still watch over and bless us.

Chapter Five

THE DOCTRINAL FOUNDATION

O NE OF THE MOST BEAUTIFUL doctrines of our Catholic faith is the doctrinal teaching on the Communion of Saints. It is also one of the most comforting truths, filled with consolation for all of us. It is the foundation of our great Novena, of our devotion to St. Ann, St. Paul of the Cross, and St. Gabriel.

Contrariwise, one of the saddest losses suffered by the Protestant so-called Reformers was the loss of the Veneration of Saints.

Saints were no longer needed, not even the first and the model of every Saint, the Blessed Virgin Mary. When a Catholic church was taken over during those calamitous wars of religion in the sixteenth and seventeenth centuries, the statues of the Saints were literally thrown out of the church upon a garbage heap and destroyed — especially their relics. The Saints were looked upon (or down upon) as obstacles to faith, distracting people from true devotion that belonged to Jesus. For us, however, the contrary is true. The Saints by example of their heroic lives lead us closer to Jesus. It is interesting to note that some four hundred years later, many Protestant churches are returning to a fresh devotion to the Blessed Virgin Mary and to the Saints.

For us, true devotion to the Mother of God, to the Apostles, and to the Saints belongs to the very first days of the Church, the Apostolic Age, and has never been lost.

In those early days, being a follower of Jesus meant putting your life on the line. Christianity was outlawed by the pagan Roman Empire. Being a Christian denied you of all privileges and protection. You could not own property, make a will, receive inheritance, or get a job. If you refused to worship the emperor, you might immediately be arrested and subject to death — a cruel death by the teeth of wild beasts; by being tarred, tied to a post, and burned to death while you supplied light for the pagan games in the Roman arena; or by crucifixion and the sword.

This, by the way, is the true origin of incense in the Catholic Church. If you offered a few grains of incense before the statue of the emperor, who was considered a divinity, you could save your life by this act of apostasy. The martyrs refused. When peace finally came in the fourth century, we offered abundant incense to the true God, Christ Jesus, and have never ceased to do so, "down in adoration falling."

And the martyrs were not a few. They numbered in the tens of thousands throughout the Empire, the known world of that time. Thus began the veneration of the Saints, these holy and heroic men and women who, for the most part, at an early age, gave up family and fame, fortune and a future for the sake of Christ. Their tombs became great shrines, centers of pilgrimages. Their relics were venerated. People sought their intercession and blessing with the relic of the Saint. The miracles followed.

At an early age the Church ordered that each altar would contain an altar stone in which were placed the relics of one or more martyrs to signify our willingness to give our lives to Jesus, who on the altar of the Cross gave His life freely and willingly for our redemption.

The truth is that we belong to two worlds simultaneously and continually: the invisible world of God and the visible world of this creation. In the first and real world, the world without end, the angels and the Saints with the Blessed Virgin Mary and her divine son, Jesus, live in joyful peace by the power of the Holy Spirit to the glory of God the Father. Into the second, the world that will pass away, by the act of God I am created an immortal spirit-soul and joined to my mortal body at the moment of conception.

Between these two worlds, the world of man and the world of God, there is continuous, uninterrupted communication, an unending exchange of love and blessing, of grace and favor. It is what the Communion of Saints is all about.

My task is to live so well in this world that at the hour of my death I will be ready and welcomed into the first world for which I was made, there to rejoice in God and to sing and dance and play forever with all the angels and Saints. That is why the famous French philosopher Leon Bloy could write, "There is but one sadness . . . and that is for us not to be Saints."[5]

But suppose that sadness hits me and I am not a Saint, not ready to see God face to face. By the mercy of God I have escaped eternal damnation and the pains of hell. What then? Again by the God who is love there is a place for me to expiate for my sins, a place of final purification until I achieve the holiness necessary to enter the joy of heaven, to be embraced by God to whom I belong. That place is purgatory.

Now the doctrine of the Communion of Saints is clear. The Church exists in three modes: the Church Triumphant — in heaven, the angels and Saints; the Church Suffering — the souls in purgatory; and the Church Militant (me and you) still engaged in the day-to-day battle to avoid what is sinful and wrong and to embrace what is good and just and true.

At the great Basilica of St. Ann in Scranton, the exchange between these two worlds, the world of God and the world of man, is made visible, effective, and actual. Every Monday and especially every July at the Solemn Novena we experience the Communion of Saints. Our prayers, our needs, our petitions in true devotion are presented to our patrons. We are blessed with the holy relics of the Saints, and our prayers are heard — sometimes more frequently than we realize, miraculously but always mercifully and lovingly.

It is not a quid-pro-quo deal. We do not barter with the Saints. The relationship is one of "my dear friend," "my protector," mother and child. We know nothing is more important in this relationship than that we imitate their virtues, model our lives on theirs to avoid the one sadness: to stray away from God, to lose our way.

There is yet a deeper meaning to the doctrinal basis of the Novena. It is one with the Communion of Saints. It is this: by Baptism we are incorporated into the Body of Christ. We are all one in Him and with Him, and consequently we are very closely conjoined, interrelated. This has great consequences. When one suffers we all suffer. When one does good we are all made better. And sadly when one gives scandal we are all ashamed; when one falls we are all brought low. There is a very positive consequence of this truth as it relates to the Novena especially in July but also every Monday: no one is alone at this Novena. Some ten or more thousand people pray over me, pray with me, pray for me. The Basilica welcomes me to the people of God. God hears the prayers of His faithful.

A final note on the doctrinal foundation of our Novena: It is biblically inspired. It is modeled upon the first and the greatest of all Novenas: the Novena that gave birth to the Church. At His ascension into heaven, Jesus commanded His apostles to remain together with His Holy Mother in prayer — praying for the coming of the Holy Spirit. For nine days they prayed this first Solemn Novena. On the tenth day the miraculous happened: the earth quaked, the thunder clapped, the mighty wind blew, and the Holy Spirit descended as tongues of fire upon the Blessed Mother and the Apostles: the Church was born.

Since that great day of Pentecost until this very day, the Novena — nine days of prayer, nine days of devotion, nine days of petition — has always had a pride of place in the Catholic Church. In July of each year, these precious nine days assume very special significance at the Basilica of St. Ann.

"It Was Definitely a Miracle: From Code Blue to Renewed Health"

Dear Rev. Cassian:

As far back as I can remember I've made the Novena to St. Ann. I always thought of her as my patron Saint, probably because I was born on her feast day in the year 1939.

It all began one day in the fall of 1999 when I just knew I had to offer up something for God. I just knew I would become sick for the Centennial year 2000.

It all started one day in January, January 17 to be exact. I went for blood work. I then went to work at my son's office. I received a call from my doctor around 2:00 p.m. that day. He told me I would have to go right into the hospital because my blood count was 4.0. Instead of going right to the hospital I went to St. Ann's Novena at 3:15. Afterward I went home, packed my suitcase, and entered the CMC Hospital. I received four pints of blood, and they began tests to determine why my blood count was so low. Every day in the hospital room I would pray to St. Ann. On January 21 I was diagnosed to have a large tumor in my colon. My surgery was scheduled for January 26. After the surgery the doctor that operated on me told me I was very lucky because the type of tumor I had usually wrapped around all your organs. He assured me everything was out, but I had one positive node and would have to have chemo.

I went home three weeks later and prayed to St. Ann and God to help me. I continued to make the Novena. I would make the

Novena every Monday and then go for chemo afterward. After my four doses of chemo, I became very ill. I was admitted again to the hospital, dehydrated. After a few days in the hospital I became worse. I was in the bathroom, and I fell down. I could hear them calling "Code Blue," and I saw all doctors around me. The next thing I knew, I woke up in Intensive Care. They then told me I had cardiac arrest. It was touch and go for a couple of days. Then I remember going to this place where I could see a figure standing and watching over me. It was beautiful. During this time I had a seizure, a stroke, and I was in a coma. The doctors told my children and friends I would not make it. Every organ in my body shut down, and I was put on IVs and machines to help my organs function.

After forty-seven hours I came out of the coma. The nurses and doctors were amazed. They told me they thought I would never make it. I told them, "Never question the power of prayer to God and St. Ann."

I connected so much with God and St. Ann. It's a shame that you have to become so sick before this happens. It taught me not to be afraid of death. Death is beautiful; it's the people you leave behind who suffer.

At the present, I have a lot of tests to go through, but I'm in good health. Thanks to God and St. Ann, I will live each day to its fullness. Thank you for letting me tell my true story. It was definitely a miracle. Thank you, St. Ann.

"A Holy, Healthy, Beautiful Baby"

Dear Father,

Several months ago I asked for prayers from you and the faithful St. Ann devotees. At that time our daughter was pregnant, despite advice from the doctors that pregnancy was almost impossible due to medical problems.

Well, I am elated to relate to you and your faithful that our daughter was blessed with a holy, healthy, beautiful baby girl in October 2001. There is no doubt that this is a miracle from St. Ann. Our daughter lost a beautiful baby, a five-year-old son, unexpectedly, five years ago.

We believe that this beautiful baby was sent to us to replace our lost angel.

Thank you,

Good St. Ann, pray for us.

"An Army Nurse in World War II"

Dear Fr. Cassian and Staff,

For more years than I can remember, my mom had a deep love and devotion to St. Ann. She named both of her daughters with St. Ann's name, her oldest, Joanne and youngest Maryann. She had her children late in life (in her late thirties) after serving her country as an army nurse in WW II. I know she was so very grateful for our health at birth. For most of her eighty-five years, she traveled to St. Ann's for the celebration of St. Ann's day. The Novena was very important and powerful to her!

Sadly, my mom died on December 26, 2000. We are very comforted to know she had a quiet and blessed death that will forever leave a lasting mark on my heart. I have enclosed a brochure which we distributed at her funeral...as I thought it might be nice to share her with you in the personal way pictures..., thoughts, and reflections can do.

Your mailings from the Basilica now come to my Pittsburgh address, under her name. If you could please continue the mailings, it will give me great comfort to know, as I face the one-year anniversary of her death...that she is being remembered at her beloved St. Ann's Basilica.

"All the Wonderful Priests"

Dear Fr. Yuhaus,

I've heard from you four times. I love hearing. You sent a beautiful signed card by you of Mother Teresa. You said you were writing a book, "Speaking of Miracles." It is always a joy to hear. My husband and I are both old and sickly, have bad arms and legs. Both use wheel chairs. We are eighty-five and eighty-three. We offer our pains to Jesus for the suffering He did for us. So thank you, we are still together. I'm at Mass every day you and all the wonderful priests at St. Ann's say the Masses. I pray for you each day.

Love and prayers.

"My Ears Are Still Attached"

Dear Father,

What a beautiful surprise, I just love the Way of the Cross Rosary from the Basilica of the National Shrine of St. Ann. You are a really dear friend. Your gift made me so happy — it seemed to brighten up this dull room and make it warm as sunshine. I have many leaflets and pamphlets with the Stations of the Cross but nothing like this adorable one. I use my prayer to St. Ann daily.

I don't know how to put in words how much I thank you for your gift. I love you, Father, and I pray God blesses you for your thoughtfulness and kindness.

I am so happy that I can now gain the indulgences at home too, as I can no longer go to church. I watch the Mass each morning on TV, and Father brings me Communion when I call him. I can do a little walking with the walker, and I use the wheelchair when needed. I do have a lot of pain each day, but I can't complain. God has been very good to me through all my illnesses. He has given me a good brother, who helps me a lot, even when dressing calls for a garment that goes over the head because I can't raise my arms. I still have my ears attached, although sometimes I feel like he pulled them off with the clothes.

So as I close I thank you a thousand times. You bring the graces and blessings of St. Ann into my heart.

"No Cancerous Tumors"

Dear Fr. Cassian,

Three years ago I was diagnosed with bladder cancer. Every three months I would go for my checkup and when the tumor was found I then needed surgery.

All the tumors I had were cancerous, and I had seven surgeries to take out the cancerous tumors.

I decided I needed more help than just the surgeries, so I turned to St. Ann to intercede for me and started going to the Novena and have the relic put on my stomach.

It was time for my next checkup after my last surgery.

A miracle took place for me by the intercession of St. Ann. I had no cancerous tumors in my bladder. I was clean for the first time. I know going to the Novena and having the relic of St. Ann put on my stomach gave me my miracle through her intercession.

Thank you for the treasure of St. Ann's Basilica, and all the Passionist priests.

"Warm Hands and Miracles"

Dear Father,

While attending a St. Ann's Novena, I had an experience I thought you would like to know about.

While at the Grotto, I was praying and holding St. Ann's hand and got a warm feeling, like a current went through my fingers and up to my wrist, and I couldn't imagine what it was. As I talked to St. Ann it happened again. I've been coming to St. Ann's ever since and told many people about this wonderful happening and have had some miracles happen since then.

"Roller Skates to St. Ann and My Wedding"

Dear Fr. Cassian,

If this story doesn't make your book we are glad to share our wonderful life together with you.

If you do put it in your book, let us know so we can purchase a copy.

God bless you. You are a special friend.

"The grass withereth, the flower fadeth: but the word of our God shall stand forever" (Isa. 40:8, King James Version).

July 2002 is just a month and year, but to me it represented a wonderful experience, as it was my fiftieth anniversary of participating in St. Ann's Novena.

It all began in 1951 when I fell down while roller-skating and a very nice young man helped me up. He asked if I would like to skate with him. I said okay, and we starting dating. This young man would later become my husband.

My new boyfriend lived two streets away from St. Ann's Church, and in July of 1952, he asked me to come to the Novena with him. Although I wasn't of the Catholic faith, I was interested in the Novena since he was always talking about attending it for ten days every July. I had never been to a Novena and didn't know what it was all about. Well, I went with him that summer and never in my life did I experience anything so beautiful. The faith and look of love in everyone's eyes making this

Novena left me with such a wonderful feeling. After that experience, I inquired where I lived and found out that a church not
too far from where I lived had a Novena, so I started attending
it there. It was so beautiful.

The years passed, and my boyfriend and I started to talk about
marriage. This was a big subject in the family as we were of different faiths. We talked over our religious differences and agreed
that if we were going to be married and be one family, we would
be going to one church together.

Well, I became a Catholic and don't regret it. My husband and
I are devoted to our faith and have been married for forty-six
years, and are blessed with a wonderful son and grandson.

When we say, "St. Ann, pray for us," we know she will. I
believe St. Ann looked over me when I was very ill and had
to have surgery. Never once was I afraid I wouldn't get better.
I never go anywhere without my St. Ann's Novena rosary. My
friends are always asking my husband and me to pray and light
candles for them at St. Ann's because we are so dedicated.

My husband has been attending St. Ann's Novena longer
than I have, since he was a young boy — about sixty-five years.
And every year he volunteers to sell candles during the entire
Novena. We never go on vacation during this time, as this is
"St. Ann's" and we go to thank her.

St. Ann has been so good to us. She has answered so many of
our prayers. We will keep making it to the Novena for as long
as we are able, and if we can't be there in person, we will always
pray to St. Ann from home. So, you can see why our being
able to attend this fiftieth Novena is such a gift from St. Ann.
My husband and I still have the roller skates that brought us
together. They are a sweet reminder of the start of our life
together, my journey in faith, and our devotion to St. Ann's
Church throughout the years. Dear St. Ann, We love you and
thank you.

"Enter Fr. John Joseph Endler"

Dear Fr. Cassian,

Perhaps you'll remember me: we met briefly after one of your mission evenings here. (Thank you for coming and re-energizing us in our faith.) I related to you briefly about a miraculous time when St. Ann interceded on my behalf many years ago. You suggested that I write it down and send it to you because it might be helpful toward a book you were writing. What follows is what I remember hearing from my mom and my Aunt Hilda when we all lived together in Scranton (St. John the Baptist Parish).

It was probably around 1941–42 (I was roughly nine years old) when it was suggested by the doctors that my tonsils needed to come out — and plans for admission to the hospital evolved. This transpired around the time of the annual St. Ann's Novena. Something that sticks with me even now is the scary feeling when that ether cone was placed over my nose and mouth. Things apparently began to happen shortly after the operation was over: I began to have trouble breathing, became cyanotic; something was definitely happening in my lungs. Ended up in an oxygen tent. The doctors told my parents that it was a "reaction to the ether." Whatever it was, things did not improve, and after ten days or so, the doctors told my parents that it was possible I might not make it through the night. This, I might add, was in the days before IVs and antibiotics, complicated by less-than-sophisticated medical knowledge.

Enter my aunt. She had been a daily visitor to the hospital throughout this ordeal (she had been widowed early in a marriage, never had any children, and became like a second mother to me). And we always walked up to St. Ann's for the nine days of the Novena. This year, the Novena was in its final days, and she came to see me after she had attended the evening service.

What she encountered in the hall outside my room was my sobbing father, who told her of the grim outlook. I know that her primary petition at the Novena was for my recovery and, now, she apparently felt the need for some desperate action. She hightailed it back to the monastery and insisted on speaking to Fr. John Joseph. She must have been very persuasive because he agreed to come back to the hospital, and I made it through the night! Recovery from then on was rapid and complete — thanks, I'm sure, to the intercession of St. Ann through her sainted friend, Fr. John Joseph.

This is the story as I remember it; and it was told and retold many times by my grateful parents and aunt.

My husband and I were in Scranton this year for the Triduum and thanked St. Ann again.

Chapter Six

THE FAMILY

~⌒∽◡∾⌒~

T HE LAST TWO WEEKS of July belong to St. Ann — not just for the people of Scranton and those who live in the vicinity of the great Basilica, but for people everywhere. And they come from everywhere in tens of thousands from every state in the union and well beyond our country. They come seeking help in their many needs: physical and spiritual for themselves, for their families, for their children. And no one leaves these holy grounds disappointed.

In this book I myself, priest and researcher, and my associate, Fr. Rick Frechette, priest and doctor, wish to share with you many great things about our faith. We see the power of faith to lift us up, to redirect our lives, to carry us over life's rough spots, and above all the power of faith to heal us in mind, in body, and in soul.

The great Novena of St. Ann belongs to the family. It is family life that makes us so successful. As you know, most of my priesthood — some thirty years — has been given over to research and analysis on the problems and issues facing us as a Church, as people of God, people of faith. I did learn a few things along the way.

Permit me to share with you some very fascinating and valuable research on family life. There is an ancient saying found among all people. It is as true today as when it was said a hundred and more years ago. It is this: "As the family goes, so goes a nation! As the family goes, so goes the Church!"

In other words you will have your fingers on the pulse of a nation if you see what is happening to American family life. You will have your fingers on the pulse of the Church if you see what is happening to family life.

And what is happening to family life in the USA and in the Church is bad news. I have said frequently in my lectures and in my preaching that the most endangered species in the United States is the American family.

Just one statistic alone frightens me terribly. One in every two marriages in the United States ends in failure. Half of all marriages go off the deep end. Broken marriages, broken promises, unfaithfulness, broken fidelity, and broken trust spew out upon this nation and upon the Church, thousands upon thousands of broken hearts, broken minds, wounded children, misguided youth, and unhappy people.

As the family goes, so goes the nation. What can we do? How can we — if we can — turn the situation around? One way only: by rebuilding, remaking, and restoring family life. And no institution in the world — no religion — so upholds, protects, and defends the sacredness of the marriage bond and the sanctity of family life as does our Catholic faith. It is what St. Ann's shrine and the great Novena are all about.

Allow me now to share with you some very fascinating research about family.

The first took place when I was in Dublin. At the request of the Bishops and major superiors of Ireland, I was researching an altogether unimaginable phenomenon: Ireland, which gave more missionary priests, sisters, and brothers to the Church than any other country, could not now raise up enough vocations to care for its own people! And be certain it was all family related.

But as I was about my work two doctors came to me and asked if I wanted to see something: their research on family life. Of course I did. The research was on pregnancy. What is happening in those first nine months of life? Much is happening, basic attitudes are already being formed, a sense of being loved, of freedom, basic fears, insecurity. All this was related to how the mother and father act and react to the life of their child.

It was a fascinating study, and conjoined to it was a study to which all scholars in the field agreed: the most important years for the formation of character, for the development of the fundamental attitudes for life, for personality development are the first couple of years. For some researchers the first year of life is the most important. Certainly by age three the basic personality, its qualities and expressions, its traits and characteristic modes are complete. And who is most important to that development? You are. Parents are. No one is more important to my life and my future than my mother and father in the first years of my life.

These studies that link medicine and spirituality have intensified in recent times, drawing the attention of professionals in both fields throughout the world. As recent as October of 2005, the Catholic Medical Association meeting in Portland, Maine, selected as the theme of its conference "The Biological and Spiritual Development of the Child." They reaffirmed the fact that the development of the mind and the brain of a child begins in the womb. Unborn children can remember even as early as the seventh month, perhaps earlier. After birth the brain develops very rapidly. It was stated that in the first three years, "A million synapses are being made every second."

A second study is most revealing. It is technically known as the study of religiosity. What it says is this: if a child even before he begins to speak develops a sense of religiosity, that child will retain that good sense all life long. What does that mean?

Religiosity is a sense of the meaning of life: an awareness of God, an awareness of others (I am not the center of the universe), and awareness of more to life than just now. Further, they say, before a child can speak he must learn the value of life, the difference between "yes" and "no," between good and bad, between right and wrong, between acceptable and unacceptable behavior. That is religiosity — and it will remain with that infant all life long.

A third was on the role of devotion to the Blessed Virgin Mary in the formation of childhood faith and the formation of youth.

The third and fourth studies are very close to home. Every Catholic should be very well acquainted with these studies from the day-to-day experiences of our faith.

The third concentrated on Catholic youth in the United States and in Canada. It was sponsored by the Knights of Columbus and cost over a million dollars to complete because it was so technical, complicated, and prolonged. The focus of the study was the relationship between youth and faith, family and the Church. What keeps faith alive in youth? What are the major problems our youth encounter to the faith? How does Church enter into their lives?

In the midst of this complicated study I was asked to include a section on the role of the Blessed Virgin Mary in the lives of our youth. Does it matter? Does it make any difference? How is it experienced? At first I resisted the inclusion of yet another area of youth life. I'm glad I succumbed to the insistence of the research team — despite the additional cost.

What did we find? The result was amazing. We found out that when youth from their infancy, even before they can talk — when they learn the Bible story of the Blessed Virgin Mary: the Birth of Jesus, the Angels and Shepherds, the Holy Night, the Magi, the Slaughter of the Holy Innocents at Herod's command, Egypt, and finally Nazareth — these youth never lose their faith. Even if they should drop out, they return to Church and their faith is stronger than before. And who develops this love and devotion to the Mother of God in them and when does it begin?

Parents do! You do! And it begins in infancy — even before your child can talk.

The fourth study I wish to refer to is a study parents and grandparents know very well. Do children who experience the influence of grandparents grow up differently than children who do not have this influence? In other words, do grandparents make a difference in the life of a child? The studies of this type have been done in Europe and America. The conclusions are the same, and every parent and grandparent knows it: the answer is a strong affirmative. The difference is pronounced. Children who have had the privileged influence of grandparents grow up to be gentler, more understanding, more generous and forgiving, and more willing to admit mistakes and wrongdoing. They relate more easily to others and are more willing to take part in civic and Church events. In fact the results were so significant that I was told to include in the application form for entrance into the seminary or the novitiate a question regarding the applicants' relationship to grandparents. I was told I would learn much about this individual by the response to the new question.

The Sacredness of the Marriage Bond

Marriage is the most fundamental and necessary institution in the world for three reasons:

1. It is God's design for the human race, God's intention from the very beginning of life on earth.

2. It is the vocation of nearly every human being — almost everyone is called to form this sacred bond.

3. Without marriage all life would cease. Our nation and our Church depend upon the solidity and the sacredness of the marriage bond.

At this point it is important for you and me to note: no institution in the world, no government, no social group so upholds, defends, protects, and proclaims the sacredness of the marriage bond as does our Catholic faith. In this we are unique in the world.

In the last ten years of his amazing pontificate, our Holy Father, Pope John Paul II, wrote and spoke over 150 times on the meaning, the value, the necessity of marriage as intended by God.

In the eyes of the Church, what constitutes a valid marriage? What does it require? What makes marriage work? Well, as you know, there are six elements. Permit me to explain each one to you ever so briefly.

First: Every marriage is sacred. Marriage is not of human making. It is divine in its origin. In this sense every marriage is made in heaven. Marriage is the common vocation — the call of almost every person. By our very nature as male and female, we are destined to marriage. Not to marry can only be because of some other special calling as to the priesthood, to the missionary life of a sister or a brother, or to perform a special service in caring for others and promoting the common good of all.

Second: Jesus restores marriage to the original intention of the Creator and bestows on marriage its highest dignity and honor by making it a sacrament. That is why marriage takes place at the altar of Eucharistic Sacrifice. That is why the priest of God is present. A Church wedding is not a photo opportunity but a sanctifying moment that is to last forever.

Third: On this element the Church is very clear, unmistakably clear. Marriage takes place between one man and one woman as God intended. Not one man and eight women, not between one woman and five men. And today, one must note with emphasis, marriage is not between two men or between two women.

Fourth: This element of a valid marriage is what makes it so successful. The fourth element is *lifelong*. Marriage is not a temporary arrangement. It is for life, and it is indissoluble. What God has put together let no one ever break apart.

Fifth: This element of a sacred and valid marriage is fidelity. For this reason a man shall leave father and mother and cling to his wife — and they shall become one — faithful to each other "until death do us part."

Sixth: The final element of a genuine marriage in a certain sense is the greatest of all six elements. Every marriage must be open to life. It is this that makes marriage so awesome, so filled with wonder, even miraculous: to give life. The highest, the greatest thing a human being can do is to give life. Under God, by God's design, to beget a new life on earth, to nourish, to protect and develop life is the highest privilege and most awesome responsibility of husband and wife.

In 2002 our Holy Father, Pope John Paul II, sent a message to every Bishop, and then the Bishops sent it to every priest and to all our people. Our Holy Father said that we are to make no mistake about the bonds of matrimony. Marriage is not an individual or private affair. It is the concern of the entire Church and of all peoples everywhere. It requires constant fidelity by day and by night. It is forever. It is indissoluble, and it is always open to life.[6]

We priests were warned of our duty toward marriage. We dare not allow a young couple to come up the aisle to the altar of God unless we personally are certain that they know what marriage is, what it asks of them, and how they intend to uphold and keep sacred the most solemn vow on earth: "I take you forever — until death do us part."

For more than eighty years St. Ann's has proclaimed these wondrous truths of our faith. St. Ann's is a family affair.

I have been asked frequently to give some basic guidelines for making a good and successful marriage and family. Is there some formula? There is. The guidelines for a happy and successful family life are four:

1. Shared faith on a day-to-day basis.
2. Prayer — the family that prays together *stays* together.
3. Quality time as a family; being there for each other.
4. Outreach — concern for others, especially those in need, the fragile and suffering in our neighborhood and beyond.

"Side Effects Are Minimal"

Dear Father,

Enclosed is an offering for a favor granted to us by St. Ann.

My husband has been devoted to St. Ann since he was a young boy, and his faith brought him the strength and courage to undergo radioactive seed implants for prostrate cancer. As of today the side effects are minimal. We feel St. Ann brought him through this very trying time.

We both go to the Novena weekly, and this brought us peace of mind.

Both of us will be forever grateful for this favor granted.

"Something from the Basilica"

Dear Fr. Cassian,

I am writing to you to ask a request. Enclosed you will find a check for $25. I would greatly appreciate it if you could have someone send a small gift from the Basilica to my aunt who is also my godmother.

My aunt is over eighty and is homebound and has been for many years. She is a diabetic and has lost her toes on her left foot. She never had any children, and her husband died about two years ago. She had a rather hard life, enduring illness and working to support herself and her husband for many years because of his mental incapacities. She endured beatings at his hand and silently suffered. I think that she is very lonely and has few visitors. I try to get to see her when I am in Chicago, but that is not very often. Sometimes it is difficult to visit with her because she focuses on her physical problems, but I know that she just needs people to listen to her. Recently she gave away her jewelry to all her sisters and nieces, myself included. I know it is mostly costume jewelry because any of her good items have been stolen by people who have been in her home to help her. It was a very nice gesture, and I know that she has not heard from many people in gratitude. I was considering sending her flowers on her name day, but I thought how wonderful it would be to receive something from the Basilica of the National Shrine of St. Ann. I would greatly appreciate if this could be done. Thank you so much. I think of her smile and surprise on July 26, the feast of her great patron, St. Ann.

"On a Rescue Mission"

Dear Father,

My husband is deceased. He gave his life on a rescue mission on March 6, 1962. I am a widow and had four children to raise and educate.

I am sorry I cannot send a donation. I really enjoy Mass every morning on TV. I cannot get to church. I walk with a cane. I had an operation for a brain tumor so they took my car away. I guess I take a lot of pills and they make me sleepy. I am really sorry I cannot help. I am on a small pension and Social Security. I do hope you enjoy your new home. You all deserve it.

My husband was the Chief and on vacation at the time, but he went on the rescue mission himself.

I also have a fractured leg. Continue to pray to St. Ann for me.

"I Am So Grateful to St. Ann's for All the Passionist Saints"

Dear Fr. Cassian,

About six months ago I was diagnosed with a large tumor on my kidney and was told that I had to have both kidneys and tumor removed. I was totally devastated. I didn't know where to turn. I am a fairly religious person who attends Mass every Sunday, and I also receive Communion on Sundays. I remember friends and relatives talking about St. Ann and even remember forty years ago attending the feast days with my aunts from out of town.

Prior to having the surgery I came to St. Ann's and prayed to her to please help me through the surgery. Well, the surgery went well even though I had cancer forming on one kidney and lost the kidney, but the biopsy showed it was all encapsulated and it was totally removed with the surgery. It's been six months, and I just had my first major follow-up. The CAT scan, chest X-ray and all blood work were clean. I am so thankful to St. Ann and all the Passionist Saints. I've been a faithful Novena attendee and haven't missed since April. I pray to St. Ann every day for helping me through this difficult time. I've made a promise to St. Ann and Jesus that I will help others by speaking of my experience in the hope I can lead them to the work of God. Nothing is greater. I've also had a blessing from the Bishop of South Africa when he was at St. Ann's, and I felt that he helped relieve some of my anxiety when I spoke with him.

God bless. Thank you, St. Ann.

"I No Longer Use a Walker"

Dear Fr. Cassian,

My name is Ree Cann. I live in Las Vegas, Nevada. Recently, I visited my sister who lives in East Stroudsburg, Pennsylvania. I had the great opportunity to visit St. Ann's. My brother-in-law was accepted as a candidate to become a deacon. This took place at St. Peter's Cathedral, which was a great honor to receive Holy Communion by the Bishop and also to shake his hand. I was so happy to be part of all this. You cannot imagine when my sister and brother-in-law took me to St. Ann's how happy and wonderful I felt.

I told my sister, Sue, that someday I would love to visit the National Shrine of St. Ann. When my grandson was a baby I took care of him while his parents were working. Every day, I would watch the Mass on TV. Sometimes it came out of St. Patrick's Cathedral in New York, and once in a while it came from St. Ann's. Being born and raised in New York City, I had been to St. Patrick's Cathedral many times. Watching the Mass from St. Ann's Basilica was even better, only because all the hymns were sung the same way as we sing in our church, which is Christ the King. That's only a part of it. So, even though Mass was over and the church was quiet, it was absolutely beautiful. I lit a candle, said some prayers, even visited downstairs. Since I walk with a cane and most of the time, use a walker, I knew it would be hard to go downstairs, but I now know that St. Ann helped me because I think she knew how much I wanted to be there.

Fr. Cassian, something happened to me after I left St. Ann's. I no longer use my walker. The reason I use a walker is because I have multiple sclerosis, lupus, and epilepsy. St. Ann's Basilica is so beautiful. There are not enough words to describe how I felt after I left. My sister owns an angel store. Being in her store, surrounded by angels has really renewed my faith in my religion. My sister and her girlfriend laid hands on me, and all my problems were somehow meaningless. I know St. Ann had a lot to do with it. I came home filled with the Holy Spirit, very little pain, and a much happier heart.

St. Ann's Basilica is truly a beautiful church, I did not want to leave.

Thank you for giving me the opportunity to express my feelings about St. Ann's.

God bless all of you.

"St. Ann Has Changed the Quality of My Life"

Dear Fathers and Brothers,

Recently, I once again petitioned St. Ann for an immediate request, and once again my request was granted. For the past twenty-five years, I have asked St. Ann for many, many favors, and my requests have always been granted. I have to say that St. Ann has changed the quality of my life by helping my family and me with some serious problems throughout the past twenty-five years. A few weeks ago, I asked St. Ann to help my daughter who was having some medical test performed, and the test results were normal. I remain indebted to St. Ann, St. Paul, and St. Gabriel, along with the Passionists who make all this possible.

"In Red, White, and Blue"

Fr. Cassian,

At one of your Masses you asked for letters of faith. St. Ann brought my son home safe and all of his soldiers. He wrote this letter to me in January 2002. As you will read in his letter, he asked me and his dad to pray for his soldiers because he knows how strong our faith is to St. Ann and if we prayed to St. Ann, they all would come home safe. Once I received my son's letter, I went over to the Basilica and asked the woman that takes care of the candles to please set up for me twenty-nine candles in red, white, and blue, and when I got there that Monday evening, she had them all set up for me against the back wall, and they looked breathtaking. I lit every candle, saying all the soldiers' names one by one. Thanks to the intercession of St. Ann, they all made it back safely except for the two young soldiers that were hurt prior to my son's letter. Enclosed is a copy of a letter I received from my son when he was in Afghanistan.

I know it is probably too late for you to use in your book, but I really wanted to share this with you.

Mom and Dad:
I need a favor. Light two candles and pray for all of us. One buddy lost his leg from a mine that blew up when we landed and then another lost his arm when a machine gun put thirty rounds in it. They had to cut it off. They flew back to California for surgery, so remember them in your prayers. Here is a list of all of us, if you could light a candle for all of us. Not all of us have parents like mine and people don't care about these heroes and that's what we are, we are heroes, cuz you don't see anyone else over here fighting scared, and excited to be here fighting for all of your freedom.

"I Came Full Circle"

Dear Father,
Everyone has a story to tell since they have been coming to St. Ann's Novena. St. Ann has interceded for me so many times over the thirty-three years that I have been making the Novena.

This particular time in 2002 when I had so many problems, I feel it was truly a miracle. My mother who had severe dementia was living with us. It was getting harder and harder to cope. I didn't feel it was time yet to put her in a nursing home, and I prayed that I wouldn't have to take the heart-wrenching step. I prayed that somehow St. Ann would intercede for me. I felt a lump on my breast. I was scared and prayed that it wouldn't be anything. St. Ann gave me the courage to have it checked out right away. It was confirmed. It was a tumor. This all happened during the nine-day Novena. I knew that because of my great faith and the timing St. Ann would see me through this. After having the biopsy, the results would come back on July 26, St. Ann's Day. It took so much courage to call. The office had a policy that the surgeon only told the patient when they came for a consultation. I couldn't wait. I told the nurse, "You don't understand, today is St. Ann's Day and I have to know." They were a little bit hesitant so they checked with Dr. Mackrell, and he gave his permission. It was malignant. It hit me like a ton of bricks. After I hung up, I began to cry. All of a sudden I had this feeling that things would work out. When I was scheduled for surgery, I knew that I could no longer care for my mother. The decision was made for me.

St. Ann interceded. My surgery was followed by nine months of chemo. One year passed. I came full circle. My cancer was cured. I had time to reflect. Cancer was a blessing. St. Ann interceded. I truly believe it was a miracle.

A Witness of Forty Years and More

St. Ann's Monastery Shrine is a holy place atop a high hill in Scranton, Pennsylvania. People from every walk of life and age including the yet unborn children in their mothers' wombs are present at this annual Solemn Novena.

St. Ann's clients, grateful for past favors, return to ask her intercession in their present needs. The sincere devotion of Novena goers makes this annual Novena a grand annual success.

The forty and more years I have ministered at this Novena have seen continual progress in the Novena's format. Implementation of Vatican II liturgical changes has enhanced the Novena.

Each day the Holy Sacrifice of the Mass and Novena Devotions are celebrated on television.

The Blessed Sacrament is exposed in the day, July 26. The rosary is recited daily by different groups. On Saturday evening a candlelight rosary procession takes place with a monstrance for public adoration. During the vigil, exposition of the Blessed Sacrament is continued throughout the night till early morning of the feast.

Confessions are heard before and after each of the five daily devotions by local diocesan priests and priests of the Passionist community.

For some years now a Passionist community gift shop is open on the Monastery premises for the convenient procurement of a rather large variety of religious articles that are blessed at each devotion. Temporary gift shops are located under tents on the spacious lawn of the Monastery.

Recent facilities have been added for the relaxation and bodily nourishment of Novena pilgrims.

Holy Mass for children and babies in their mothers' arms is an exciting spiritual event on Saturday morning at ten o'clock.

For more than forty years, I've witnessed so much that indeed is miraculous. St. Ann's has become an inseparable part of my Passionist priesthood. (Fr. Clement Kasunskas, CP)

Chapter Seven

THE CHILDREN

T HE WELL-BEING OF CHILDREN is so important to Christ that the harshest words He ever speaks in the Gospel refer to those who would harm a child — when He says that anyone who would harm a child would be better off with a millstone tied around his neck and thrown into the sea (Mark 9:42).

We know that the future of the human family is determined by how we treat children today. Children are our tomorrow. What is sown in their hearts and souls will take deep root in the future and be determinant of the directions the human family will take — toward God or away from God, in an embrace of life or an embrace of death. Children are the seeds of the future. They are the seeds of immortality since through their innocence faith is passed on from generation to generation until the last days. This truth is not lost on the powers of evil, the forces that oppose God and life. It is no wonder at all that evil sets its mark in a merciless way on children, and tries to destroy them through the evil choices of other human beings.

Very shortly after the peace and joy of the birth of Christ in Bethlehem, we see the bloody massacre of innocent children (Matt. 2:16). The heart-wrenching wail of Rachel's grief for her children echoes in a bone-chilling way down through the long ages (Matt. 2:18). It is still heard by the mystics of our day. This outrageous violence waged against tiny babes had only one goal, to rip Christ out of the human family and banish Him forever. The same savage forces would reappear again thirty-three years later, attempting the same annihilation of Christ from the human family through a bloody crucifixion (Acts 2:23–24). In the Bible the peaceful birth of Christ and the slaughter of innocent children, events that are absolute contradictions in meaning, are separated by mere paragraphs. In our liturgical calendar, just three days after Christmas when we remember the Holy Innocents, the Church forces us to look at the blood of children so that we might be vigilant of the ways that evil, in an attempt to destroy God, attempts to destroy children today.

When I received the first American newspaper in Haiti describing the uncovering of child abuse in the Church in Boston, on the same front page as the article exposing the abuse, in bold headlines was the unbelievable statement that the Supreme Court of the United States was upholding the right to possess child pornography. Only paragraphs separated these two contradictory expressions of the law of our land that would on one hand rightly prosecute pedophiles, but on the other protect child pornography. This shows the insidiousness of evil. It shows how schizophrenic our laws are when they are built on arbitrariness.

Catholics make up almost a third of the population of the United States. Should seventy million Catholics, a third of our nation, tolerate such a ruling? Couldn't we eradicate protection of child pornography from our laws? We certainly could — if we were convinced of the existence of evil, convinced of the enormous power our moral choices have, and if we were united. The sad truth is that many Catholics are disconnected from the sacraments, spend little time with the Scriptures, and have allowed our culture to water down their convictions.

Can we expect to find deep meaning and happiness in life when we disrespect life itself? Pope John Paul II so strongly referred specifically to the cultural embrace of death in the developed world and urged us look around to see its deadly fruits, which are obvious to anyone who wants to see. Without the conversion of heart necessary to see that a unique human person is created in the womb by God, that this person walks through life to find full union with God through natural death, and that this sacred journey from beginning to end is a divine right — without seeing this and acting on it in justice, how can we ever know peace? When our house is constructed on sand, on such a huge fault line as disrespect for human life at every level, how can we not expect the slightest tremors to make our house fall completely? Signs of collapse are everywhere. Total disintegration is certain for us unless we respect life from beginning to end, from conception to natural death, and live fully the Gospel of Life. Good St. Ann, shelter the unborn in your loving arms, be the protection of abused and abandoned children, and help us find conversion, pardon in right living.

The suffering of children in the world is enormous and unbelievable. In many countries there are child slaves, children exploited in brutal sweatshops, children abused in sex industries and prostitution — especially in countries economically underdeveloped and marked by blatant corruption. Often people travel from the developed world to satisfy their lusts with these children. Starvation of children and the countless deaths from easily treated illnesses give sobering testimony to the extent of worldwide poverty and its harvest of death. Some international organizations claim that as many as twenty thousand children die around the world each hour. These children have names — I have held many of them in my arms over the last twenty years. Marie and Jean and Patrick and Mackenson and Esther and James. Their bodies weigh in your arms; their agony weighs in your heart. They die from starvation because they weren't lucky enough to be born here where we throw food away every day from nearly every table in the land. They die of easily treated illnesses because they weren't lucky enough to be born here to enjoy the protection of vaccines and immediate medical care. They die of violence and abuse because they weren't lucky enough to be born here, where for all of our faults, we have protective laws and strong, even if delayed, enforcement of them. When you hold a dead child in your arms you never forget it, and the number twenty thousand makes you shudder.

I think of Mackenson, a young boy I found in the poorhouses of Port-au-Prince — out on his own in the barren courtyard, under a sheet. His face was rotted from cancer and he was so ashamed of his monstrous look and rotten smell that he wouldn't talk to anyone. I built a bond with him slowly until he trusted me enough to come to our mission hospital. In time he made friends and became playful again. He rediscovered his childhood. Once he grabbed my hand and felt the hair on my arm and asked me why God gave me feathers. I took him outside and had him feel a chicken — so he'd know the difference between feathers and hair — and not think I was a big turkey! One day at Mass he blurted out, "I want to hear God talk! I want God to tell me if I'll get better." I was stunned and didn't know what to say. The Scriptures tell us that at such moments we shouldn't worry, it will be given to us what to say (Luke 12:11–12). Suddenly, I heard myself telling Mackenson that the world is full of people who talk too much and don't do anything, and that God is the opposite — if we want to know what God is saying we just look at what he is doing. I explained to Mackenson that it was clear from what God had done already for him that God wanted him to have friends, the hospital as his home, good care of his wounds and his pain. And as for getting better, there was no answer except the assurance that the same God who wanted Mackenson to have good care, a home, and loving friends would not let him down no matter what was in store. Before I left Haiti to care for other children, Mackenson said he knew he would die, and when he did he would pray for us from heaven.

Through compassion, what a great thing God has done — he has given playful childhood back to a ten-year-old boy with a terrible disfiguring burden, has surrounded him with love, and has helped him face death without fear, with a promise of compassion for us when he is before God! God enters human history through compassion and works wonders.

I also remember Alex, a little boy at our orphanage, and how his eye began to swell.

When it was apparent the problem was serious, a biopsy I was able to get done in New York revealed that he had a dreaded eye tumor called rhabdomyosarcoma. I went to my knees to beg God's help, and Alex was accepted into a cancer center for children in Florida for a $250,000 yearlong treatment of his cancer. After a year of chemotherapy and radiation, which he tolerated beautifully — the best treatment any child in the world could get — his cancerous eye was shriveled and sunken. We discussed removing it surgically, since it was dead, to prevent infection. Instead we decided to leave it alone to serve as a space filler for his socket. So his shriveled eye was sewn closed. A half-year later, Alex returned to Florida for his checkup, and the doctors cut the stitches over his eye to reevaluate whether the dead eye should be taken out. When they opened the eye to have a look, they were not the only ones looking. Alex was looking at them through that one shriveled eye! Not only was Alex cured from the dreaded tumor, but that eye that had been so filled with cancer, bombarded many times over in radiation therapy, and had been sewn closed for a half a year — that very eye had been restored to sight! God gives grace in abundance, good measure and flowing over (Luke 6:38). God enters human lives through compassion and works great wonders.

So what do we do, with the help of St. Ann? We commit ourselves to oppose any evil that destroys children or childhood. We respond generously to the needs of children in crisis. We keep in our prayer an awareness of crucified children around the world and our fervent desire to save and defend them. We insist that the globalization of the world, well underway, be formed on a solid base of morality that defends and protects children.

Above all we must each of us commit ourselves to treat with love and friendship and instruction in God's ways every child with whom we come into contact. A hundred years from now, it won't matter what your profession was, what your favorite color was, what kind of car you drove, or how much money you had. The only thing that will matter in a hundred years is how you treated a child today.

Good St. Ann, grandmother of Christ, pray for all the children of the world, especially those in the most distress.

Chapter Eight

THE MYSTERY OF SUFFERING AND EVIL

I arise today
through the strength of heaven:
Light of sun,
radiance of moon,
swiftness of wind,
depth of sea,
firmness of earth.
God's wisdom to guide me,
God's shield to protect me,
from all who would wish me ill,
afar or anear,
alone or in a multitude.
Against every cruel and merciless power
that might oppose my body or my soul.

— *The Breastplate of St. Patrick*

THESE WORDS are over fifteen hundred years old and are attributed to St. Patrick. They express a deep conviction of God's compassion — that God, right from our rising to meet a new day or the beginning of any venture, surrounds us with the comforts of creation, with guidance and protection. They express the conviction that our lives not only mean something to us, but mean even more to God, who is ever eager to help us in our trials and preserve us in life unto eternity.

Fifteen hundred years of wars, famine, plague, and disasters have not shaken the conviction from the Christian heart that God cares for us with a passion. We believe that the petitions we bring in honor of St. Ann are important to God who will help us — petitions that represent our sorrows, our tragedies and burdens, and our dreams.

It is the mystery of evil that makes God's compassion necessary. If we were still in Eden, God's generous love, which created us and gave us a place in a harmonious world, would be enough for us. Once paradise was lost, a new expression of God's love was born — tender pity for the suffering (passion) of the people, and a desire to suffer with them (compassion) in a transforming way. The mystery of evil, which crouches ever near like a lion and is ever ready to destroy (Gen. 4:7), found its entrance into our lives through the free choice of human beings. Adam and Eve embraced sin, and how quickly evil took hold and required of us that we return to dust (Gen. 3:19). The Book of Wisdom makes it clear that God did not create death. God takes no delight in the destruction of the living (Wisd. 1:13). The Book of Genesis tells us that we return to dust because of the great original sin of pride chosen by Adam and Eve. How quickly the sin of pride gave way to the abomination of murder, and worse of a brother killing his own brother — and then to the lies to cover it up (Gen. 4:6–10). The story of evil goes on and on through the ages, ever gaining in strength. The passing of the millennia showed the last century to be the bloodiest and most destructive in all of human history, and our new millennium has begun with murderous terrorist attacks in our country, and unbelievably shocking evil in the sex abuse scandal in our own Church.

91

Ageless evil makes its entry into human affairs always the same way, through the choices made by people. How clear it is that free choice is the doorway through which evil takes its hold.

After the devastation of September 11, which shocked the whole world, the Pope decried the fact that the authors of the terror used obedience to God as their justification. He stated that it is eminently clear that any organization that turns its own followers into missiles launched to kill the innocent has a worship of death as the core of its soul. This is absolutely opposite to the worship of the God of Life.

Cruel and merciless powers killed countless innocent people on September 11 and thereafter.

A child might rightly ask why the prayer of St. Patrick could not ward off these tragedies. The answer is simple and yet all-important: because Almighty God chose to share almightiness with human beings; God surrendered power over evil by giving that power to us. Why did He give the power to us? Because the crown of creation, the highest imitation of the Creator, would be in the free choice of the human person to offer love to God and neighbor and to reject evil. And so the choice between death and life, between good and evil became ours and continues to be ours.

This makes it all the more extraordinary that we still believe in God's compassion after all these centuries.

What sustains our belief in God's compassion is that we come to feel and know that God enters into our suffering in a transforming way. While God did not undo the consequences of Adam's sin by destroying death, God became *Compassion Incarnate* by becoming one of us, in the person of Jesus Christ. He showed us how to live and how to die, and in the brutal way of His dying He refused to let evil enter into His choices or attitudes. He fought off despair, revenge, hatred, and the will to brute power. And by making of His dying a willing sacrifice offered in compassion even for His assassins, He transformed death from being the enemy that annihilates each individual life to the doorway to the fullness of life in eternity. It is still death, but it is also now, amazingly, something else.

God's transforming work is constant. After the September 11 tragedy, Pope John Paul II said that it was essential to trust that great love would be born from great suffering, that with hearts open to God's grace it can always be so. The same admonition was made by Pope Benedict XVI after the devastation of Hurricane Katrina. And truly the responses across our country, across our world were tremendously inspirational and showed the best of what human beings are capable. When we do not find a miraculous solution to our burdens, we find another gracious help. If we use our free will to choose to let God into our agony, then God accompanies us eagerly and helps us transform our burden from being merciless power that might destroy body and soul into a power that brings blessing and benefit to ourselves and others.

In my work in Haiti I see terrible poverty daily. I see death, sickness, misery, filth, and violence. I see the desperate masses, who are half starved and without clean water to drink or a place to lie down, without any chance for help when they are sick or wounded. They are brought to us often in wheelbarrows, burned, shot, stabbed, feverish, half dead — and usually they have borne these maladies for days without relief, and we are often their only hope.

Not long ago when we were in Wharf Jeremy, we heard an unbelievably wild lament. Many children were crying inconsolably. You knew immediately it was not the cry of someone who was just punished or who had fallen down. It was a chorus of deep, soulful screaming and crying. We walked until we found the shack where it was coming from. In all my life, I have never seen a more pitiful sight. Five little children whose father was shot dead, left alone by the mother who had gone to find the body on the street, were out of their minds with grief. They were rolling on the dirt floor, covering themselves with mud, ripping their clothes and wailing and screaming, a sound that would shake your bones. One was clutching a dead kitten. I did my best to console them, to hold them, to talk with them, but there was nothing I could do to penetrate their frenzied grief. Finally we went out to find the father's body and there it was, baking on the street in the tropical sun, with the wife wailing at its side. We put the body in our truck and took the wife with the body to the morgue and gave her some money to do the official paperwork at the city morgue and to buy something for the children and some money for the funeral. You can imagine we go through money like water, facing these situations one after the next, and I dread the day when finances will not allow us to take an active role in helping with these problems. That day will be a huge challenge to faith, because we will be present but helpless ... as helpless as the poor people themselves.

I didn't sleep all night. I could not get the pathetic scene out of my mind or the pathetic lament out of my bones. The next day, after Mass at the orphanage, we went back to Wharf Jeremy with seven chicken dinners. We sat in the little sweltering shack and talked with the children as they and their mom feasted on chicken. I made it a point to learn their names. This time they came to me, and sat with me, and we were able to express our sorrow to them and to try to give them an experience of goodness, of friendship, of love to counterbalance and offset the horror. It was deliberate on my part to offer a humane and spiritual medicine as close as possible to the moment of horrific suffering. It must have worked. The mother offered all the children to me, and the children begged me to take them. But such solutions are far from ideal.

Since then we have completely relocated the family out of Wharf Jeremy, and thanks to good friends in Scranton, Pennsylvania, they are in a safe and simple house with their mom, and we will get all the children in school.

People often ask me how I can believe in God after seeing all these terrors. I always answer that I have no problem believing in God. God does not will these things. God finds them abhorrent. God wants us to have life, in its fullness and unto eternity. Human beings cause poverty. It is the result of politics and economics based on greed and power. Once again, human choices have given evil a stronghold, showing itself in the form of supremely undignified misery. I have more trouble believing in people than in God.

How does God transform the dreadful situations of life into something else? By waiting for the human heart to open freely to grace, and then making an abode in that heart. I see this happen frequently with illness in my work as a physician.

The Scriptures tell us clearly that God makes an identification with the sick. God seeks union with the sick in a preferential way. The prophet Isaiah describes a man we refer to as the Suffering Servant, who is considered to be the prefigurement of Christ (Isa. 53). Isaiah sees him as so disfigured that he doesn't even look like a man, so bent by his burden that he doesn't have a human form. But the prophet sees something else as he keeps his gaze steady in contemplation — and this is what makes Isaiah a prophet. He sees that the disfigurement is caused by *our* illnesses and that the burden is the weight of *our* sorrows. God has made our sin, sickness, and sorrow precisely God's own.

And we hear this message with more forceful clarity in the Gospels, when the disciples ask Christ when they ever saw Him sick and cared for Him. The answer is a direct identification without the slightest hesitation. Whenever we care for someone who is sick, no matter how insignificant they may be in our eyes or the eyes of the world, we have cared for Christ directly (Matt. 25:35–40). "Truly I tell you, just as you did it to one of the least of these who are members of my family, you did it to me."

There is an even more extraordinary revelation from St. Paul. He tells us that our sickness or burden can become an apostolate, a holy work of God. Paul exhorts us to join our sufferings with those of Christ, to make our suffering a sacrifice, offered willingly and in compassion for the benefit of others (2 Cor. 4:17; Col. 1:24; Rom. 8:18–19).

By God's grace, the meaning of sickness changes as the sick person becomes a preferred abode of the Living God, as those who care for the sick person care directly for the Christ who "did not regard equality with God as something to be exploited" (Phil. 2:6), and so the sickness becomes a holy work in union with the sacred passion of Christ, for the benefit and salvation of many.

Recently in Port-au-Prince, a man named Hubert, nearly dead from AIDS in Mother Teresa's home for the dying, begged me for the medicines available for his disease in the United States. He was emaciated, full of infection, and covered with sores. He asked me if the medicines could give him even two or three more days of life. Why would a half-dead man, on a cot in a poorhouse, with a death sentence written all over his body, and surrounded by multitudes of equally desperate people ask for two or three more days of life? You would think he would ask me to end his life mercifully.

The answer is that he has become a tabernacle of the living God, and he feels it. God is near him. God is in him. God is doing something new with and for him, and he can't help but glory in the mystery that engulfs him. "A day in your courts is better than a thousand elsewhere" (Ps. 84). For this man, two or three more days would be a fabulous gift.

The interior of the Basilica of the National Shrine of St. Ann

St. Ann and her child, the Blessed Virgin Mary, Upper Basilica

St. Paul of the Cross, Father and Founder of the Passionists, Upper Basilica

The Consoling Angel: Garden of Gethsemane Grotto

Grotto: St. Joseph the Working Man, dedicated to all volunteers at St. Ann

Daily Mass: National Telecast from the Basilica

The Rose Garden Grotto: Our Lady of the Angels

*Evening Stations of the Cross seen from the Grotto of Gethsemane
and the Grotto of St. Joseph*

As we come to the Basilica with our intentions, needs, and hopes, I certainly hope for each of us that we find miraculous solutions from God. But if we don't, another wonder awaits us. We can open our hearts to God and enter into a deep transforming union born of God's grace. Then the burden, when it does not leave us, will also not destroy us, but rather will become a source of blessing. For this to happen we need the right attitude as we offer our petitions. We need an eagerness to enter fully into the mysteries of our faith. We need a willingness to pay the pearl of great price for the transformation we seek. We need the compassion to make our burden become a sacrifice for the benefit of the human family as we unite our sufferings with those of Christ. If we do this, we will not be disappointed in our encounter with our compassionate God, and the ancient prayer of St. Patrick, in praise of God's compassion, will ring true once again today.

Good St. Ann, help us be ever more servants of God's compassion!

"A Nickel for the Poor Box"

Dear Fathers and Brothers,

Please accept the attached calligraphy piece as my thanks for all you do to help make the St. Ann Novena and the Basilica a truly wonderful and satisfying experience.

Also, please accept my thanks to St. Ann for all she has done for my family and me throughout the many years I have attended these services.

When I was a youngster, I remember my Mom holding my hand and taking me to the Novena with her. She would always give me a nickel for the poor box, but before the Novena was over I almost always dropped the coin, and it would roll away under the seats. I always worried if whoever found it would be sure to put it in the box for the poor people. Even at that young age I remember praying to St. Ann for favors, and she always helped me.

I am now a senior citizen — she is continuing to help my family and me. Most recently she helped family members come through operations safely and with good results, favorable biopsy results, peace of mind, and better working conditions. I will always sing her praises.

Please keep up the good work.

"I Was an Unwed Teenage Mother"

Dear Father,

In the 1950s there was no such thing as a single parent. I was an unwed teenage mother who had to give her baby up for adoption. It was a closed adoption, but I always prayed that my son's identity would be revealed to me. After forty years, in the year 2000, I finally not only had his identity revealed to me, but my identity was also revealed to him. We met on St. Ann's feast day. When I found out his adopted mother's name was Ann, I knew St. Ann was watching over my son for forty years. I'm happy to say I have a close relationship with my son and his family. I will never stop thanking St. Ann. I have been devoted to St. Ann since my childhood.

"Two Months Premature"

Dear Father,

My daughter was born two months premature. She weighed four pounds. She was on oxygen and a feeding tube. She was in the neonatal unit for one month. She then contracted bacterial meningitis and a strep B infection. She was taken to the Children's Hospital and put on life support. She was blessed with

St. Ann's oil and a St. Ann's medal was put in her crib. The priest at St. Ann's said Masses and prayed for her every day for one month. She received a total healing with no side effects. Her hearing, eyes, and heart are all normal. She is now five months old and attended her first St. Ann's Novena and was blessed with the relic of St. Ann. We remain devoted to St. Ann.

"This Illness Is Still Kicking Me Around"

Dear Fr. Cassian,

Please convey my thanks to the Passionist priests and, if the opportunity presents itself, to Bishop Timlin, for the healing Mass of just over a week ago. My computer broke down or I would have corresponded sooner.

I hope all your brother priests realize how important it is to me and I suppose to many of the sick that you stand in and fight with us in this battle with illness. This illness is still kicking me around! Thanks to all of you for striking a blow against it. It will take many blows apparently to win the battle. So you must be trained in endurance.

I don't know if the warrior mentality is theologically correct for healing, but I think it is apropos because what sickness does to us is, I think, well described in terms of a fight. These illnesses are "kicking our butts," or whatever more colorful expression you can think of for getting beat up as in a one-sided boxing match or other sort of fight. And while illnesses can possibly strengthen our spirits in the long run, they are also wearing away at our spirits. I don't need anyone to tell me something good will come of illness. I want someone to fight with me and to fight for me when I run out of faith and energy. Particularly the latter.

At St. Ann's I find the help I need.

"I Wanted to Make a Good Confession"

Dear Father,

I don't know if you would remember me as you hear confessions from so many people — but on Monday morning after the Novena you gave me confession. I had told you I had cancer and wanted to make a good confession. You did just that, and I was so happy and filled with emotion that it took me a while to settle down. You asked me if I prayed, and I do all the time — the rosary, Chaplet of Mercy, and about an hour of prayer in the mornings. My husband and I have been making the Novena at St. Ann's for years and have received many favors. We have purchased a brick at the third Station of the Cross. I feel that was so meaningful for us, and from time to time we do have Masses said by the Passionist priests. St. Ann is very near and dear to us. I want to thank you so very much. You can never know how much that meant to me. I really don't like to go to confessions where there are a dozen priests and a hundred people rushed through, so my husband and I have been going to confession at St. Ann's. I have had good confessions at St. Ann's, but this is the first time I told them my problem and wanted to make a confession of my sins I may have forgotten to mention previously. I know this is a long letter and sorry for that, but please know that I will pray for you every day and thank you for helping me so much. I close with all my love, thankfulness, and respect.

"From California with Love"

Dear Father,

Back in the early 1950s I attended Marywood College (and for three months I was blessed by being in their novitiate). I kept a little black notebook for favorite little sayings, poems, etc. I still have it.

Last Sunday I happened to find St. Ann's program on our TV from Scranton(!), Pennsylvania. Again today I did the same. Today had your Fr. Provincial, Fr. Kristofak interviewed — we get it maybe a week later, and on Sunday here.

I used to go to visit St. Ann's Monastery — and the Novena was on the radio. Passionists used to give retreats at Marywood. I remember going to confession at St. Ann's.

In my little notebook I have many quotes from Fr. Sweeney, CP, such as: "Any grass shrivels up as soon as fire touches it; so likewise, do all our sins burn into nothingness when we ardently love God...." "Cling to the book that helps you to love God...." "We can never thank God enough that there is an end to everything here. Were it not for the end, what would we ever do with our sorrows...?" "The thorn we have carried in our hearts all through life will, if we have willingly accepted it, from the hands of God, blossom into a rose at the moment of death...." Etc., etc.

I am blessed with the memory of so many dear priests and sisters. I thank God for all. I can still remember thirty-nine IHM Sisters! I was there when that dear priest, Fr. Daniel Lord, came to Scranton his last time. He held a Day of Recollection for the four Catholic area colleges at Hotel Casey, and he returned for the University of Scranton graduation — as speaker. He died of cancer not too long afterward. What a joy he was. I have several of his books — his autobiography, *Letters to my Lord*, and wonderful *His Passion Forever*.

My husband is a teacher and a convert. We have five sons and three daughters and two granddaughters and two grandsons. I still visit my first-grade sister, Sr. Felice Hickey, retired, at Marywood.

Today's sorrow over the priests who have broken their vows so very long ago is a cross for all of us. No doubt our beloved Holy Father and Mother Angelica are two of God's beloved who are suffering for the Church. Of course "all will be well" (as Jesus told Lady Julian), and Jesus said the gates of hell would not prevail against His Church — so we must all repent, to quote Fr. Groeschel. God help those victims. God help those priests, God help all of us — His Church.

May St. Ann pray for the Passionists, one hundred years in Scranton! I will always remember all the Passionists in my prayers. Please pray for my children and grandchildren. St. Ann is very dear to us.

"That Most Wonderful and Blessed Basilica on the Hill"

Dear Fr. Cassian:

I want to thank good St. Ann, the Blessed Mother, St. Paul of the Cross, St. Gabriel, as well as you and all the priests and brothers at St. Ann's for another favor granted, the latest of hundreds, and to ask for your prayers for our safe deliverance in the days ahead.

First, the latest favor: A few weeks ago my wife awoke me one Friday morning with the horrific news that she was going to the hospital for a breast biopsy. I shall never forget that morning, or the overwhelming sense of despair that engulfed me. She had known about it for weeks, but did not tell me until the very last minute to spare me weeks of worry. But that also prevented me from contacting the Basilica for prayers. Needless to say, I spent all that day at the hospital in prayerful conversations with good St. Ann and the Blessed Mother, asking that we be spared the horror of breast cancer, or given the strength necessary to carry that cross. You can imagine our relief when the surgery ended and the surgeon told us all preliminary signs looked good. A few days later the laboratory report confirmed the good news.

Thank God, St. Ann, the Blessed Mother, St. Paul of the Cross, St. Gabriel, and all of your wonderful Passionists.

Thank you so very, very much for this and all of the other prayers on our behalf and on the behalf of all the faithful who find so much help and solace at that most wonderful and blessed Basilica on the hill. We pray for you every day. God bless you all and the outstanding work you are doing.

"A Very Sick Little Boy"

Dear Father,

Matthew, at four years of age, was diagnosed with a Wilms tumor. He was taken to Philadelphia Children's Hospital. He was hospitalized and had surgery to remove a kidney. Matthew was a very sick little boy but a real trouper, very brave through his whole ordeal.

The prayer line for Matthew spread far and near, so many people praying for him. His grandparents, living near Scranton, were able to make Novenas to St. Ann, and we truly believe that St. Ann interceded with her grandson, Jesus, on behalf of Matthew.

When Matthew was in remission and came to visit, we took him to St. Ann's to meet some of the priests. While waiting outside the gift shop for Fr. Cassian, Matthew, a very shy little boy, surprised us by turning to Fr. Cassian and hugging him to give thanks to St. Ann.

Thank you, St. Ann.

"It Is Such a Blessing"

Dear Fr. Cassian,

You especially make the daily TV Mass so interesting to me because you are very devoted and pious in your delivery of the liturgy and sermon. You speak so informatively and admiringly of the different Saints whose feast days we happen to be celebrating at particular Masses.

At my age — eighty-five years — it's so good to hear you recall some of the stories of the Saints that we used to hear about way back when I was a little girl and also to hear about some Saints that I never really knew about until you've introduced them to us at Mass. How I enjoy hearing you tell about them all and also many of the people in the Bible.

As you always say, Father, I look forward to having you and all the folks at St. Ann's bring the Holy Mass and the Holy Eucharist right into my home where I am now homebound. But it is such a blessing to be able to receive spiritually the Body and Blood of Jesus, my Savior, while you devotedly pray over me.

I just wanted you to know how much I appreciate your coming. You are a blessing to me.

"I Was an Orphan"

Dear Fr. Cassian,

It gives me much pleasure to be contacting you in this way. I know that you maintain a busy schedule. You are all so friendly. (Is this one of the prerequisites for being a good Passionist and/or an associate?)

Before proceeding on any further, I will give you a little bit of my personal background so that you will understand me a little better and know where "I come from." I am a seventy-four-year-old homebound amputee. My wife works during the day. I have four children, three boys and one girl. I am a retired college professor and librarian. I lost most of my left leg in July of 1983 and have been retired since that time. I was the head of the English department at Laval University in Quebec City, Quebec, in Canada. I was also a school librarian for seventeen years. While I would not recommend that anyone lose a leg in order to get to retirement, for me it has turned out well enough.

I have always lived by the religious idea that THY WILL BE DONE!!! I was an orphan, adopted late in my teens, but God has always watched over me. As you probably know, the Blessed Virgin Mary is the mother of orphans. (Possibly that is the reason that I learned to say the rosary at a very early age, and STILL do today.) I also watch Masses as much as possible as well as wear the scapular and do THE WAY OF CROSS. (My wife, Pauline, says that it's almost like being married to a priest.)

Incidentally, my wife and I are originally from Rhode Island although we have lived in other places. Someday I would enjoy a trip to your monastery to meet "you-all" in person. Who knows what the future holds?

Vera mentioned to me that you teach Church History at one of the local colleges. I thought that you were a retired Passionist provincial or something of that order. I enjoy listening to your homilies because they are so enthusiastically religious. Your speaking style reminds me of the way one of my confreres (from Belgium's Louvain University) at Laval University would discuss topics, very culturally. It's a shame that your sermons must "per se" be short, due to the limitation of time. Your affection for the homebound is overwhelming. GOD BLESS YOU FOR THAT! We thank St. Ann.

Chapter Nine

ALL LIFE IS SACRED

‹~~~›

T HE COMPASSION that God has shown for us since our loss of
Paradise, the compassion of Christ whose very blood won
our redemption, the compassion of the Holy Spirit who showers
us with spiritual gifts until the end of time, all place us under
a tremendous obligation to be missionaries of compassion. We
need to bring love where it is most difficult to bring, precisely
because love is most needed.

Dying is probably the greatest work of our life. In fact it can
be said that our whole life is a preparation for death. We need to
bring compassion to dying, and to death itself. When I work in
the poorhouses of Port-au-Prince, even though I can't possibly
attend to all the people who are there, I am very much aware
that they are doing this great work of dying — trying to reconcile
their lives, their hearts, and their spirits in preparation for death,
and I am in awe that it is all going on around me.

Respect for their last *agonia,* their last chance to give themselves completely to God and to grace, makes me eager to
offer the sacrament of Anointing — that special sacrament to
strengthen them with grace in their great struggle. The same
respect also makes me eager to bless their bodies when they
have died.

In Haiti you can imagine that the poor are not embalmed.
They are laid out all together in a small shed. Of course, the
shed is not air conditioned, and there is no way to keep flies and

maggots from coming in and no way to get the stench of death out. They lie there until a government pickup truck comes for them; then they are thrown in a pile in the back and driven to a common grave where they become feast for pigs and vultures — in a place whose Creole name "Titanyin" means "smaller than nothing." It is a terrible reality, but it is the reality of many people in the world. In fact, most of the world's people live in abject poverty and know such an end.

We pray for the dead in that little shed in order to honor their bodies. The psalmist says, "For it was you who formed my inward parts; you knit me together in my mother's womb. I praise you, for I am fearfully and wonderfully made" (Ps. 139:13–14). Even though the bodies are now rotting before us, it is still true that they were created by God, and that gives them a tremendous dignity that carries over even into their disintegration. We give witness to that dignity, even for a few minutes, and we protest against the terrible indignity of their poverty in death, by kneeling at their side and offering our prayers. We bless them with holy water, to call to mind their Baptism when they first died with Christ sacramentally (Rom. 6:3–11). Now they reach the end of the cycle and die in the body, to share with Christ the Resurrection. We bless their bodies because they record their whole life story. Each wrinkle, each scar is like a sacred letter on leather parchment, telling a fabulous story of tragedy and heroism, precious to them and precious to God. We pray for them because they belong to the Communion of Saints — they are still in the community of God. We express this belief each time we recite the Creed. We pray for them because, as St. Thomas Aquinas tells us, we can still relate with the dead through charity. Why is this so? Because just as the soul is the life of the body, charity is the life of the soul, and Scripture tells us that only three things will last: faith, hope, and charity — and the greatest of these is charity (1 Cor. 13:13). We bring our compassion to the dead, and we honor them in a final work of love.

Meditation on death is powerful. I can think of three times when I thought I was facing my death. Once I was in a terrible truck accident in Honduras. I thought I was going to die. My truck was totally destroyed, but I walked away without a scratch. Another time I was in an airplane in El Salvador when we went into a thunderstorm, got caught in air currents, were struck repeatedly by lightning, and we were thrown up and down repeatedly by wind. A third time, in Haiti, I was pulled out of my pickup by soldiers who threw me against a wall and put guns to my head, neck, and back.

What I remember most about all three incidents is that I was not afraid. That was a great surprise to me. I often wondered why I was not afraid, and my conclusion is that my charity to the dead was returned to me. The dead I frequently remember in charity were showing charity to me. The Communion of Saints stood by me, and helped me to face these difficult situations calmly. Thank God they all had a good ending.

I knew a young man named Tony who was murdered a year ago. You can imagine what a devastating blow that was to his family. After his body was recovered and brought home, his father dreamed, that very night, that he saw Tony, and they spoke. Not with words, but with their hearts. His dad told him how devastated they all were, and that Tony's mom especially was lost. Tony replied, "I have begged God for her." When I was finally able to talk with Tony's mother, she herself told me of a great grace she had received through Tony. She said she knew on her own she would never have been able to be free of hatred for her son's killer, and she knew that hatred would destroy her, and rob her of peace, until her own death. She knew it was a grace to be freed from hatred and to feel an abiding peace because she knew it was nothing she could achieve on her own.

She bore no hatred and sought no revenge for the murderer of her son. Tony had begged God for her, and her heart was eager for that saving grace.

The Communion of Saints is an awesome reality. We gather at the Basilica because we believe that St. Ann, who once walked on this earth as a human being, now belongs to the Communion of the Saints. She lives to make intercession for us. She can beg God for us. She can help us open our hearts to saving grace.

Our technological world presents us with a grave danger — a culture whose fruit is death. We need to bring compassion to this death as well. We spend most of our time with things we have created and which dominate us — TV, computers, virtual realities, the Internet. We are caught in a trance whereby we believe ourselves to be absolute masters of the world, and like Adam we leave no room for God and want to eat of the fruit of every tree. We tamper with the beginning of life — the mysterious beginning — even though it is known by science that at conception, or within days of it, the genetic code for a fully human, individual person is present. Yet we destroy that person — at the first only for exceptional reasons, then for convenience; at first only within the first months of pregnancy, and eventually even at full term in the abominable practice of partial-birth abortion. Now we are trying to tamper with life at the other extreme — when it is marked by the mysteries of old age, illness, and death. Not only are we unable to see any value in struggle or suffering, but we are less and less able to tolerate a "useless" life. We have developed the urge to end the life of the terminally ill in euthanasia, which is already legal in Oregon. It will become attractive in other states, and eventually its victims will be not only the exceptional cases, but all who have nothing to offer in a utilitarian and commercial society. When the sacred beginnings and sacred endings of life have been exploited, what can we expect of every moment in between? Life becomes more and more empty of meaning, of spirituality. Is it any wonder marriages fall apart? They stand on nothing. Is it any wonder that children are shooting each other in our schools? That suicide is a leading cause of death among teenagers and fast becoming a leading cause of death among children eight years of age and older? Their lives are empty shells. Is it any wonder that there is so much depression and addiction in our nation? We have smashed the spiritual foundation on which God invites us to build our lives together. We don't even know what "together" means anymore. We live in the empty and meaningless wasteland of a world we have fashioned in our own image instead of God's.

We need to protest the death of spirituality in our technological society. We need to protest it at the level of the grass roots, by restoring it there. We must remember the dead in prayer and remember them in our visits to the cemetery. We must rejoice that we are creatures of a provident God, and break the delusional trance that we are the masters of creation. We must vow to oppose any tampering with life from conception to natural death, and be open to all of life's mysteries. We must work to protect all the other creatures of our universe, and the created world itself, by not letting them be sacrificed for technological advancement. We must look the hard realities of life squarely in the face; we must look at death and not deny it. We must not be afraid of its revelations, its challenges, its power. Death is no longer an enemy. It is not even just a natural ending of life. It is the very last step in a long journey toward salvation. This is why St. Paul says so beautifully that, for the Christian, death is gain (Phil. 1:21–23). God's compassion reaches to death and beyond, giving us a place in the Communion of Saints, and clothing us in glory.

Good St. Ann, mother of the Mother of God, pray for us sinners now, and at the hour of our death. AMEN.

Chapter Ten

HOW FAITH HEALS

T ODAY, MORE THAN EVER BEFORE, a new understanding of
faith has captured our minds. Perhaps it is due to the
enormous amount of suffering and evil we have experienced
in recent times: the natural disasters like the tsunami in Asia;
the terrible hurricanes like Katrina and Rita; the devastation
of war, especially in Africa, in Iraq, and the Near East; the
horrendous and continuous assault upon precious life in the
womb; the crushing pandemic of AIDS; the increase in violent
crimes, particularly among the young. The new understanding
of faith today responds to our urgent need — the need for healing. In every disaster mentioned above, it is faith that brings
healing.

In the wild 1960s, faith was mocked — laughed at. It was
something for old men and women. It was good for children.
Not so today. To be without faith is to be alone and lonely in a
confused and disturbing world. It is a sickness.

The healing power of faith is the power of Jesus ever active,
ever present. Jesus said to us so beautifully, "Do not be afraid.
I will not abandon you, I will not leave you orphans. I, myself,
will be with you always until the end of time."

You cannot turn a page of the Gospel without finding Jesus
healing every kind of affliction: the lame, the crippled, the blind,
the mute, the leper, the possessed, the brokenhearted, the disturbed mind, the tortured soul. He healed until late at night and

111

before sunrise, the sick, the injured, the frail, all pressed against His door. He healed them all!

Jesus is with us. He is with us today. He is in His Church. He is in our homes. He dwells in our hearts. And He continues to heal directly and in a special way through the intercession of His Saints — as we see in this great devotion we have to St. Ann, grandmother of Jesus.

How does faith heal? Faith heals in five ways. Let me tell you the ways.

First, faith heals miraculously. A miracle is something that cannot be done in any human way. There is no human causality — no human explanation. And miracles are not so very rare. They are happening every day somewhere in the Church. There are hundreds at Lourdes and Fatima, Guadalupe, Knock in Ireland, Loretto in Italy. Here at St. Ann's, many have claimed to be cured miraculously. It is why I am writing this book.

Second, faith heals uniquely. Faith heals where nothing else was able to work. This is especially true of various forms of addiction — alcohol, drugs, sexual addiction, gambling. In the famous AA program, Steps One and Two begins with the admission of not being able to do it alone, but by trusting a higher power beyond me — the power of God to heal. Faith heals uniquely in various forms of mental illness and depressions. The famous psychologist Carl Jung, in a letter to Pope Pius XII, admitted that in his thirty-five years of practice, he cannot recall a single case that the healing didn't come through the intervention of faith. Faith heals uniquely.

A recent book by Dr. Dana King, called *Faith, Spirituality and Medicine*,[7] explains numerous studies that show that those who believe in God and commune with God regularly through the rituals of their faith make out remarkably better than their peers who are on medicine alone! We have always known the power of faith in healing. The Passionists have always known it — our very Rule states that our lives give witness to the truth that the compassion of Christ is the remedy for all the world's ills.

The third way faith heals is the way priests know best because they experience the healing continuously. Faith heals mercifully. We, priests, witness the miracle of Divine Intervention — the miracle of grace.

What am I talking about? I'm talking very clearly from experience. Here is a man trapped in sin: sinful ways, sinful thoughts, sinful habits. A person who has abandoned God, turned on the Church, lost his faith, his decency, his honor, is locked in sin — ten, twenty, thirty years. There is no power on earth that can turn that person around. There is no power on earth that can lift that man out of his prison of evil.

Suddenly, unexpectedly, he turns and finds his way back to God, back to Church, back to his family. Faith heals mercifully.

What made that possible? You did. I did. It is the intercessory prayer of good people who bring the sinner the grace of healing from sin and sinful ways — as St. Monica prayed for her sinful son, Augustine, for nineteen years. It is the power of our great Novena, and it happens year after year, sometimes week after week.

The fourth way faith heals us is by enabling. Faith enables us to get through the worst times in our lives and not be crushed. For example, the death of a child, the loss of a husband, financial disaster, the loss of friends. Without faith, we are lost. Faith heals by enabling us to endure great suffering and pain and not lose hope. We have so many examples: Mother Teresa is outstanding. St. Padre Pio, our own Cardinal O'Connor, Cardinal Bernardin to name a few — each one suffering to the last day. Above all these we have the heroic example of Pope John Paul II. The power of faith enabled him to carry a hard and heavy cross, especially during the last years of his holy life.

Faith heals in yet another way: sustainingly. Faith sustains us. When I was a young man, my father said to me, "Listen, boy, do you know what you are doing? Do you know what 'forever' means? To vow forever to be pure, humble, to be obedient, and never have money to call your own — forever? Do you know what you are doing?" Pop was right. You can never do it if you depended on yourself. But God calls you. God sustains you. Faith is a healing power that sustains us for the long run.

Every married man and woman knows what I am talking about. "Until death do us part." Faith is a day-to-day, healing power in our marriage, our home, our family. Faith heals the broken heart, the broken home, the broken parish, by sustaining, renewing our hope and our trust.

Rightly do we celebrate our faith as we sing:

> *Amazing grace! How sweet the sound*
> *That saved a wretch like me!*
> *I once was lost, but now I am found,*
> *Was blind, but now I see.*

Faith heals in five ways:

Miraculously: An instant cure, an instant gift, a blessing granted that has no human explanation. It is a gift by direct, divine intervention.

Uniquely: When no other way can be found, suddenly a door opens, a light goes on, a way is found. Life is renewed.

Mercifully: The sin-filled man or woman locked in the prison of sinful ways, sinful habits, sinful beliefs is lifted out of his or her prison by Divine Mercy.

Enablingly: In the midst of pain and suffering even every day for ten to thirty or, as with Padre Pio, fifty years, I am enabled to carry the Cross with confidence and hope and even with a mystic joyfulness.

Sustainingly: In the most difficult circumstances of life, near impossible to human understanding, I am sustained by the God who made me, who loves me and stands by me, still holding my hand.

This book is filled with marvelous witnesses to the healing power of faith.

Chapter Eleven

STANDING ON HOLY GROUND

⁓⤳⤳⤳⤳

T HE GREAT BASILICA of the National Shrine of St. Ann and
the Passionist monastery adjoining it rest on holy ground.
Throughout the world, the Catholic Church has recognized certain places as special places of faith and devotion. They are
designated as shrines. The ground on which they stand is holy.
We may rightly ask, What makes this ground so holy? Why is
it special? We see the effect the shrine has upon people. We
see the change it makes in the lives of those who frequent the
shrine, and indeed we see many miraculous events take place as
reported in this book.

But we did not answer the question: What makes a shrine
holy? Why is this holy ground? The answer is clear. This is a holy
place because God makes His presence felt here in unmistakable
ways. It's what so many people say to us: "I can't stay away. The
moment I arrive on these holy grounds, I feel God's presence.
I feel the goodness, the love and the mercy of God come upon
me. I am at peace."

The confirmation of this divine presence and power is mea-
sured in "feet" — in terms of thousands of feet over these past
eighty years and more. The feet of toddlers taking their first
steps on these holy grounds. The feet of children running up
and down this holy hill from the Grotto to the food stand and
back again. The vigorous and agile feet of youth ready to climb
to the moon, the tired feet of hard-working parents struggling

to make a good life for their children, and the slow but deliberate feet of Grandma and Grandpa who just had to come to say, "Thank you, St. Ann," yet once again. It is like the good lady in the Gospel who suffered a hemorrhage for seven years and exhausted all her savings until she heard of Jesus. She knew in faith if only she could get near Him, stand on that holy ground, even just to touch His garment, she would be healed. Despite obstacles she came to the holy ground where Jesus stood. She made that touch with the Divine. She was cured.

The Passionist community that serves this shrine knows what it is all about and why we are standing on holy ground. They know well it is through no merit of their own that these marvelous things happen at St. Ann's — even though they pray every day to be less unworthy of these divine blessings and favors. They know well that their very presence on this holy hill was made possible by divine intervention. When nobody, not even the best-qualified mining engineers in the region, believed the monastery and church could be saved from the continuing mine subsidence, the worst the area had seen, and everyone — priests, brothers, employees, and others — were under police order to evacuate, the small community prayed through the night. At dawn they requested that the engineers take one final check down the mining shaft. They went down. They came up. They were new and different men. The engineers themselves believed it was miraculous: three huge boulders never seen on previous examinations locked firmly and directly beneath the church and stopped the slide to disaster. St. Ann took care of her own.

The priests opened the doors wide to welcome warmly all who came to these holy grounds seeking help in their many needs. They resolved to proclaim by word and example the Good News of forgiveness, of healing, of peace. They would provide, even on a daily basis, ample opportunity for clergy and laity to receive the great sacrament of Reconciliation (confession of sins) and the supreme gift of Christ, His most precious Body and Blood in Holy Communion. They would make the great Novena, in July and every Monday, a living source of encouragement, inspiration, and hope for all peoples — Catholic, Protestant, Jewish, and Muslim — affirming in this visible way the dignity of every person and the appreciation of what is good and noble in every race and culture. Increasingly from the time of the fearful and nearly disastrous mine subsidence until this day, the grounds of the National Shrine of St. Ann have been declared holy.

His Holiness, Pope John Paul the Great, had great respect and affection for the Passionist priests and brothers. In 2000 in a letter to the whole community honoring St. Paul of the Cross, he said, "The work of the Passionists has always been a source of great consolation to me." When in 1994 through the intervention of Achille Cardinal Silvestrini, he learned of the great work the Passionists were doing at St. Ann's in Scranton, he willingly determined to raise St. Ann's to the dignity and the privilege of a Basilica following a two-year period of investigation to determine the accuracy of all that was said about this holy place, these holy grounds.

Just a few years ago as he canonized three new Saints at the great shrine of Our Lady of Loretto, he stated that this is what the Church is all about. It is all about holiness of life. He went further then to declare that the greatest thing you can do for your nation is the greatest thing you can do for your Church: lead a good and holy life.

And this is what the Basilica of the National Shrine of St. Ann is about. People of all walks of life come here to touch the Divine, to taste and see the goodness of the Lord. They leave these holy grounds renewed in faith, confirmed in grace, blessed in countless ways. Yes. Even miraculously!

"I Feel at Home"

Dear Fr. Cassian,

I would like St. Ann's to accept my small contribution in the amount of $100 for its debt reduction effort.

St. Ann's has been an integral part of my family probably since the Passionists came to Scranton early in the twentieth century. My eighty-one-year-old mother tells the story of her mother carrying her from Tripp Park to the monastery to have her bowlegged legs blessed to give her the strength to overcome the condition. She also talks about how St. Ann's was always there for them in time of trouble as well as joy. She remembers the fun she had singing in St. Ann's shows and how the people at St. Ann's did everything with gusto and dedication.

St. Ann's has also always been important to me. I can remember going to the Novena as a child (although back then the ice cream at the concession stand and being able to light a candle all by myself were the highlights of the Novena). And now, forty years later, I still try to get to at least part of the Novena each year.

When I go to St. Ann's now, whether to the Novena or to a regular Mass, I feel at home. The Passionist community exudes a dedication and devotion, a spirit of community I haven't seen elsewhere. But more importantly to me, I feel welcome, even as a stranger. St. Ann's opens its arms to everyone, even to those who, like myself, feel evermore left behind by the Catholic Church. With you I am at home.

"Help Fill the Void"

Dear Fr. Cassian,

Once more I write to you first to request your prayers as we enter the Advent season to help fill the void of my loss of my wife.

I am one of the millions of viewers you speak of who wait anxiously for you and the Mass each day. I deeply appreciate the daily Mass. Your opening remarks and homilies are great sources of nourishment of the soul to me.

In your thanksgiving Mass you mentioned a religious order based in Montreal, Quebec, Canada, whose rules are based on thanksgiving. I believe they are the Missionary Sisters of the Immaculate Conception. May I have their address so that I might contact them?

I wonder if I may call on your wisdom and experiences as a loving servant of God. As I indicated, I am a devoted viewer of the daily Mass who has spent his life in a wheelchair due to having been born with cerebral palsy.

I was married twenty-eight years to Mary and we have raised four children to adulthood, but since her passing I have been extremely lonely and unable to discern the will of God. Can you give me any suggestions and insight into recognizing the voice of God? I await your book to help fill the void.

"As of This Moment I Am Freed"

Dear Fr. Cassian,

Maybe it's because I've already experienced cancer (I'm forty years old) that relationships in my life have come to mean more than *anything*. I was in touch with you last year to thank you for your presence and enthusiasm and love for those you prayed for — through the daily Mass television program.

Somehow, I wanted to let you know that God in his Mercy and Providence (neither of which we can hope to understand fully) has permitted my life to be extended. (My oncologist told me I had about two weeks left when I started treatment.) As of this moment, my cancer has been reduced to a near remission state; I am "freed" from the couch, where I stayed for 8 months, and I actually just started back to work, part-time, with my husband. (I do some small secretarial tasks for him.)

You had mailed me a Mass card last year. It contained, besides the picture of you with Pope John Paul II, an extraordinary prayer by John Paul about illness, separation, and death, and their impact on the family. Ironically, my treatment took me out of town, away from my family except on weekends, for another 8 months. I kept that card and kept reading that prayer about separation. I shared it with several of the other cancer patients I was in treatment with.

I just wanted you to know that your acts of kindness have been far reaching.

Love in the Holy Family.

"Merciful Consolations"

Dear Father,

This message has given me peace so many times. I can testify to the fact that God is so individual, yes, with each of us, in what He gives us to bear. His merciful consolations have not been lacking!

Your Cross

The everlasting God has in His wisdom foreseen from eternity the cross that He now presents to you as a gift from His inmost Heart.

This cross He now sends you He has considered with His all-knowing eyes, understood with His divine mind, tested with His wise justice, warmed with loving arms and weighed with His own hands to see that it be not one inch too large and not one ounce too heavy for you.

He has blessed it with His holy Name, anointed it with His grace, perfumed it with His consolation, taken one last

121

glance at you and your courage, and then sent it to you from heaven, a special greeting from God to you, an alms of the all-merciful love of God.

—St. Francis de Sales

"Hugs and Kisses"

Dear Uncle,

I thank you for praying for me during my hour of suffering and doubt. I praise and thank God for putting you in my life. I am still recovering from a virus, but our worst fears have been put at ease. I am very blessed with the everlasting faith of our family. You are at the heart of that faith and love. May God's grace always shine bright in your soul. You touch so many lives, yet make each of us feel so special. You truly are a man of God with many precious gifts. I also want to thank the priests and brothers of St. Ann's. Please let them know I think of them as part of our family as well. The Padre Pio relic you sent to me is oh, so sacred. It remains very close to me. Thank you so much for it. Please take care of yourself, as much as you care for all of us. I sometimes get afraid that you do too much, but I know you are under God's watch and protection. I hope to see you soon.

Know that I love you and pray for you always.

Hugs and kisses.

"I Lost My Firstborn"

Dear Fr. Cassian,

St. Ann and our Blessed Mother answered my prayers. My son Michael wasn't feeling well after Thanksgiving week. He was tired and had tingling in his hands and feet all the time. He went to the doctor and he took blood tests and he had a spinal tap to see if it wasn't a viral infection. They were all fine, but the CAT scan showed something in his head that the doctor didn't like.

I prayed so hard that it wasn't anything life threatening. You see I lost my firstborn son, Martin, when he was nine years old. He drowned on us at the end of my street as I have the Great South Bay at the end of my street. I don't think I could live through another loss of a child, so I prayed that St. Ann and our Blessed Mother would help him and they did. Even though it was diagnosed as multiple sclerosis, it isn't life threatening and with treatment he can live a full life, thank God. So I promised the Blessed Mother and St. Ann I would send a regular donation to thank them so much for answering my prayers, and God blessed me with two more sons too. So I have four children and love them all so much. I saw you today when I watched St. Ann's Novena. I was so happy to see you again.

"Soon His Hands and Feet Would Have to Be Cut Off"

Dear Father,

Dabitur quid loquamini.

It is strange that these Latin words come to my mind today, having been buried under eighteen years of memories. While on retreat in the final days of preparation for our ordination as priests, we were reminded of Our Lord's promise in the Gospel of Matthew that in critical moments of life we would find the words we needed to speak. We would not stammer or hesitate. "For what you are to say will be given to you at that time" (Matt. 10:19).

Today I stammered. Today I hesitated. I could not find the words to tell the five-year-old Julio that soon his hands and his feet would have to be cut off. No, such words do not exist. Not for a five-year-old child. Such words could not be given.

Poor Julio had a defect in his heart. Last month, while undergoing surgery to correct it, he went into shock and heart failure, and it seemed death was certain. In the fight to save his life, he was given drugs to keep his blood near his heart, to keep his heart pumping vigorously. In such instances the hands and the feet, legs and arms give up most of their blood for the good of the whole body. In Julio's case, the hands and feet never opened their vessels again to receive their gift of blood back.

Pascale Duc, a volunteer from Switzerland, and Sister Dorothy Ammon from New York were with Julio. I met them in the hospital along with Bob and Tish, two wonderful friends with whom I study medicine. Together we prayed. Together we anointed Julio's hands and feet with the sacramental oil of our faith. We begged God to restore the flow of life-giving blood. Surely it must be a scandal to God, to see a five-year-old child face life without hands or feet. Especially in Haiti.

In spite of our prayers, Julio's hands and feet died, and hung like withered leaves on a living tree. Julio was scared and withdrawn. His hands were kept wrapped so he could not see them, but he caught a glimpse of them one day while being bathed and was filled with terror. We had all witnessed, time and again, horrible suffering in the Haitian children we serve, but for some reason Julio's fate shook us more profoundly than others. I found myself questioning the worth of the sacraments, the value of prayer, the kind of God who would not intervene on behalf of this poor child, and wondering if surviving isn't sometimes worse than death.

But then the Spirit who I felt failed me with words helped me to see something very clearly. It would be wrong of us to misread God's promise. It would be wrong of us to draw back from life and its challenges, and isolate ourselves in disappointment and cynicism. It would be wrong to withdraw from the sacraments and prayer because they did not work the way we hoped and expected. To do these things would make our souls wither as truly as had Julio's hands. We would be lifeless branches hanging off of living communities.

The Spirit helped me see that God's promise still stands. The sign of God with us is that the blind will see, the mute will speak, the lame will dance for joy, but not necessarily in the way we expect. The Spirit helped me see what I can do, what we can do, to make the promise a reality. I can promise God that as long as I am alive, Julio will receive the help that he needs to live well and be productive and happy. I believe I will see Julio walk one day, and then run, and then chase a ball and throw it back to me. I believe on that day I will stammer again. I believe that God will send to us (indeed God already has) someone who will be able to provide Julio with artificial hands and feet, and teach him how to use them. Yes, all this is better than withdrawing in bitterness. All of this *is* the fruit of our prayer. We embrace life as it is, we accept it, and we sacrifice with love for a promised future.

I'll close this letter here. I want to go back and reread that verse in the Gospel of Matthew. It has new meaning for me now. The Spirit helps us to see clearly, and thus it is also given to us what to do. *Dabitur etiam quid agatis.*

Fr. Rick Frechette, CP

"St. Ann, St. Ann, Send Me a Man"

Dear Father,

Enclosed is a donation in thanksgiving for the many, many favors bestowed on us throughout our lifetime and the happy days as children we spent at St. Ann's. We'd have a dinner prepared by the long-gone wonderful women of the parish and spend the day there.

125

Later at Marywood we'd try to attend a devotion in the evening as we prayed,

> St. Ann, St. Ann,
> Send me a man
> As quick as you can.

And she did! A good one. Don't forget she has a sense of humor.

St. Ann's continued to be my comfort and strength when my husband was killed in action in Germany on the first birthday of our son. Returning to the area to be with my parents I found peace after a long time.

Please pray for my son and his wife, and for my grandsons. Please pray for me. I have cancer.

I have full confidence in good St. Ann.

"We Come Back Every Year"

Dear Fr. Cassian,

This Monday, my husband and I attended the 5:30 Novena Mass, heard you say about a book you would write on people who have experienced miracles that happened to them through prayer to St. Ann. I heard you a few years back mention this at one of the Monday Novena Masses. I never did do anything about my miracle that I experienced through prayer to St. Ann. For years before moving to Florida (four years ago) Mario, my husband, and I attended every Monday Novena Mass, also every July nine-day Novena in honor of St. Ann. Also, to say we never missed Novena Masses, now we try to come back every year which thank God we did attend the nine-day Novena, also for the length of our stay we attended every Monday. Now I tell you which I truly believe was a miracle happened to me on a Monday Novena Mass to St. Ann which we attended a few years back. Hurting my back in the seventies at work and had trouble and pain until one Monday at Novena Mass to St. Ann, walking into Church had trouble making steps, shuffled my feet not able to lift my legs, to sit it was an effort, could not kneel. During the Novena Mass I prayed and continued praying all during Mass. After Novena Mass was over went up to get blessing from St. Ann. Before I left and started to go out the doors, I had no pain, was able to lift my legs without pain. To me that was a miracle. I thank St. Ann every day and night, say my prayers every day from St. Ann's Novena book. To me I cannot thank St. Ann enough. All I can do is pray to her every day.

P.S. Father, please excuse my writing. It must be my age. I'm seventy-six and will be seventy-seven in January. Another senior moment: I forgot to mention that I was married at St. Ann's by Fr. Kevin McCloskey. We miss him since he passed away.

"No Further Problems with My Heart"

Dear Father,

This is a short letter explaining a wonderful gift I received during attending my first summer Novena to St. Ann in 2004.

I had not been feeling well during the days of the Novena. I had a bad weak spell and also developed an irregular heartbeat. I was very worried about myself. My doctor sent me for special noninvasive tests which all came back normal.

I truly give credit to wonderful St. Ann for praying for my healing. Since that Novena, I had had no further problems with my heart.

My neighbor, who did not know I wasn't feeling well, gave me a prayer card at that time for Blessed Francis Xavier Seelos. I did pray to him along with St. Ann for healing.

I am now very devoted to St. Ann.

"There Was Only a Tent"

Dear Fr. Cassian,

I am writing to you to let you know of two miracles my mother had from St. Ann. By the way, she said she went to St. Ann's when there was only a tent on the property.

She always refused to go to an eye doctor because she said they could tell if anything was wrong with you by looking in your eyes. But one day when a friend was over she told us she could see nothing out of her right eye. We immediately called Dr. Pugliese, the eye specialist, and scheduled an appointment for her. The doctor said the cataract was so heavy he feared her sight would be gone completely, but he would operate and remove the cataract. She blessed her eye every day with St. Ann's oil while waiting for the operation, and to the doctor's surprise, her sight was wonderful. She didn't even wear glasses afterward.

Another miracle she had was regarding a lump found in her breast. The biopsy was taken, and we had a two-week wait for results. I was so nervous, but she was calm and blessed herself each day with St. Ann's oil. When we returned to the doctor's office, the nurse said, "Anne, you are so lucky."

She knew right away it was a miracle from St. Ann.

"I Prayed Day and Night"

Dear Father,

I am writing to you about a miracle that happened almost three years ago.... On June 14, 2003, Father's Day, a young man took sick. The young man was given no hope for survival. He was medicated with sedation and placed on life support for six and a half weeks.

During the six weeks, the doctor informed us that if he did make it he would suffer from brain damage, but they could not tell us how severe it would be. Plus all his organs had shut down. . . .

In July during the Novena to our beautiful St. Ann, I took the young man's photo with me. I prayed day and night to her for a miracle. This is the outcome: the young man had three-fourths of his lung and two ribs removed during his surgery. The day of the feast he was taken out of ICU and placed in a respirator and from there to a rehabilitation unit to learn how to walk, feed himself, and gain strength. Blessed St. Ann gave us a beautiful gift, his life.

Now after two years he is able to walk, talk, and take care of himself. He only suffered minimal brain damage, so that he cannot remember what happened to him and sometimes has problems with his short-term memory.

Father, I wanted to share this with you, because it also brought me back to the Lord and all the Saints and martyrs.

"My Father's Personal Experience"

Dear Fr. Cassian,

Very recently my uncle, Joe Connor, asked that I write what I remember being told of the miraculous healing that my father, Hugh Connor, received through the intercession of St. Ann and send it to you.

I am happy to relay exactly what I recall being told by him, and by members of my dad's family, about the events that took place when he was a young child suffering from acute rheumatic fever. Please edit my words in any way you feel necessary, and I hope that you find his story worthy of inclusion in your writings about the miracles attributed to St. Ann.

God bless you in your undertaking, and for all you do to bring devotion to St. Ann to so many.

St. Ann and the Connor Family

I have been privileged to be the eldest of twenty-nine grandchildren of Charles and Mary Connor, who were the parents of eight children; and also the eldest of three children of Hugh, their son, and Mary Connor. From the time I was able to remember, St. Ann has been revered by the entire Connor family, whose home was in West Scranton practically in the shadow of St. Ann's Monastery, now known as St. Ann's Basilica. The family's strong devotion to St. Ann was rewarded at an early age when another son, Charles, at the age of sixteen entered the Passionist community at Dunkirk and was ordained Fr. Julian Connor, CP, in 1936.

Over the years many marvelous stories of miraculous healings, favors granted, etc., through the intercession of St. Ann were relayed by family members, but none impacted me more than the one concerning my own father, Hugh, and his personal experience of the powerful intercession of St. Ann.

At an early age Hugh developed acute rheumatic fever and spent months in bed, weakened by this malady and suffering the effects of a very high fever and extremely swollen and painful joints. It has been told by family members that even the sheets touching his body became unbearable. A most frightening aspect of this condition is the damage ordinarily done to the heart of a child suffering from the disease. The family experienced grave concern because of the probability that this would be the case with Hugh.

At a particularly critical point one day, Fr. Julius Boyd, CP, came to the Connor home and spent the afternoon invoking the intercession of St. Ann, and blessing Hugh with her relic and holy oil. Miraculously the very next day he rallied and quickly regained his strength and vitality, with no indication of any ill effects or heart damage. St. Ann's protection had seen him through a most serious illness and restored him to good health.

Hugh lived a full and wonderful life, never losing his devotion to St. Ann, and never ceasing to recount the "miracle" that Fr. Julius procured that afternoon as he prayed to St. Ann on his behalf.

Late in his life he experienced a few heart attacks from which he recovered, and later when diagnosed with terminal cancer the physician treating him mentioned that he would most likely not suffer the final rigors of the cancer because his heart would not withstand it. But the strong heart, that good St. Ann had protected, held out for two and one-half years before finally resting, and Hugh at last was to meet the mother of Our Blessed Lady and the grandmother of Our Savior face-to-face.

Chapter Twelve

BE NOT AFRAID

~~~

THESE THREE WORDS, "Be Not Afraid," hold much meaning and have such great significance for all time but especially for our troubled times. They come to us from heaven and were first spoken by an Angel. Our redemption began with the words, "Be not afraid."

When the Virgin Mary was frightened and so disturbed by the words of the Angel, the Archangel Gabriel said to her, "Do not be afraid, Mary, for you have found favor with God" (Luke 1:28–30).

Jesus used these words frequently throughout his ministry. At three o'clock in the morning when the Apostles were in danger of capsizing in the turbulent Sea of Galilee, Jesus came walking upon the water. They were terrified. Surely it must be a fearsome ghost. Jesus called out to them, "Take heart, it is I; do not be afraid" (Matt. 14:27).

When Peter was confronted by the reality of Jesus on the Lake of Gennesaret, Jesus said to him, "Do not be afraid; from now on you will be catching people" (Luke 5:1–11).

And when, after his horrible crucifixion, Jesus rose from the grave and suddenly appeared to Mary, Mary Magdalene, and the disciples, his first words were, " 'Peace be with you.' They were terrified. . . . He said to them, 'Why are you afraid? Look at my hands and my feet and see that it is I, myself' " (Luke 24:36–38).

Finally, on the morning of His Ascension into heaven, gathering His Apostles before him for the final time, Jesus, with warmth and reassurance said, "I am with you always, to the end of the age" (Matt. 28:20).

Few people in our day could understand the full significance of these words as did our beloved Holy Father Pope John Paul II. That is why he could write this message to all of us:

> There must grow in the consciousness of all peoples and nations the awareness that there is someone who holds in his hand the destiny of this passing world...someone who is the Alpha and Omega (the beginning and the end) of every individual and of all human history. This someone is love: incarnate love, crucified and risen love! It is love unfailingly present among us. It is eucharistic love, the abiding source of community. Only the one who embodies this love can say with fully guaranteed assurance: "Be not afraid!"
>
> Perhaps more than ever we need to hear the word of the risen Christ: "Be not afraid!"[8]

Pope John Paul needed to hear these words when, by the age of nineteen, he had lost his mother, his brother, and his father and was homeless and all alone in this world. He needed to hear these words when he was hunted by the Nazis, run over by a truck and left for dead. He needed to hear these words when he worked by day in a stone quarry and studied secretly by night to prepare for the priesthood. He needed to hear these words when as Archbishop of Cracow he confronted the Communist invaders of his country with the Cross of Jesus. He needed these words with painful urgency when he dropped in his own blood in St. Peter's Square, his body riddled through with the assassin's bullets.

Pope John Paul did hear these words all through his life. It was no surprise, then, when in the evening of the October 22, 1978, when I saw him step for the first time into the great balcony of the Basilica of St. Peter, I would hear him call out to the entire world, "Be not afraid. Open wide the doors to Christ!" Twenty-six years later as he lay dying in the papal apartments of the Vatican, he reassured us again and again, even though he knew death was moments away, "Do not be afraid! Do not be afraid."

These words were cherished by everyone as a precious legacy of the beloved pontiff Pope John Paul II. But someone more than anyone else grasped the full importance of these words. As the closest collaborator of the Pope for more than twenty years, Joseph Cardinal Ratzinger was privileged to have these words addressed personally to him many times. "Joseph, be not afraid." That is why, the morning after his election Wednesday morning, April 20, 2005, Pope Benedict XVI addressed these words, the very first of his pontificate, to the College of Cardinals that elected him:

> At this time, side by side in my heart I feel two contrasting emotions. On the one hand, a sense of inadequacy and human apprehension as I face the responsibility for the universal Church, entrusted to me yesterday as Successor of the Apostle Peter in this See of Rome. On the other, I have a lively feeling of profound gratitude to God who, as the liturgy makes us sing, never leaves his flock untended but leads it down the ages under the guidance of those whom He Himself has chosen as the Vicars of his Son and has made shepherds of the flock (cf. *Preface of Apostles I*).
>
> Dear friends, this deep gratitude for a gift of divine mercy is uppermost in my heart in spite of all. And I consider it a special grace which my venerable predecessor, John Paul II, has obtained for me. I seem to feel his strong hand clasping mine; I seem to see his smiling eyes and hear his words,

at this moment addressed specifically to me, *"Do not be afraid!"*[9]

And then Pope Benedict XVI went on to say on that same occasion:

> I am thinking in particular of the young. I offer my affectionate embrace to them, the privileged partners in dialogue with Pope John Paul II. I will continue our dialogue, dear young people, the future and hope of the Church and of humanity, listening to your expectations in the desire to help you encounter in ever greater depth the living Christ, eternally young.[10]

On the following Sunday, April 24, 2005, before a million people gathered in St. Peter's Square and beyond in the homily for the solemn Mass for the inauguration of his Pontificate, Pope Benedict XVI gave us this admirable, warm, and moving exhortation:

> We are living in alienation, in the salt waters of suffering and death; in a sea of darkness without light. The net of the Gospel pulls us out of the waters of death and brings us into the splendor of God's light, into true life. It is really true: as we follow Christ in this mission to be fishers of men, we must bring men and women out of the sea that is salted with so many forms of alienation and onto the land of life, into the light of God. It is really so: the purpose of our lives is to reveal God to men. And only where God is seen does life truly begin. Only when we meet the living God in Christ do we know what life is. We are not some casual and meaningless product of evolution. Each of us is the result of a thought of God. Each of us is willed, each of us is loved, each of us is necessary. There is nothing more beautiful than to be surprised by the Gospel, by the encounter with

Christ. There is nothing more beautiful than to know Him and to speak to others of our friendship with Him.

Only in this friendship are the doors of life opened wide.

Only in this friendship is the great potential of human existence truly revealed.

Only in this friendship do we experience beauty and liberation.

And so, today, with great strength and great conviction, on the basis of long personal experience of life, I say to you, dear young people: Do not be afraid of Christ! He takes nothing away, and he gives you everything. When we give ourselves to Him, we receive a hundredfold in return. Yes, open, open wide the doors to Christ — and you will find true life. Amen.[11]

And if there is one message that echoes across the holy grounds of the Basilica of St. Ann, it is these same words: "Do not be afraid."

People come here from all over the United States, from Canada and Central America. They come with heavy hearts and saddened spirits, carrying great burdens of pain and sorrow, of disappointment and disillusionment with deep concern for their family, their marriage, their children, and their friends. The most consoling message they hear is "Be not afraid." You are not alone. The Lord is with you. His Holy Mother and His Mother's mother know you and your needs. The entire worshiping community is with you. "Do not be afraid."

As this book testifies, your prayers will not go unanswered. Through the intercession and the loving care of our glorious patron, St. Ann, and the prayers of St. Paul of the Cross and St. Gabriel, the door will open for you. You will find the way. You will be lifted up and embraced by the God who is love. "Be not afraid."

COME VISIT US

~~~∿~~~

To arrange a tour from March 1 to July 26, or from September 1 to Thanksgiving, please write:

> Very Rev. Fr. Rector, CP
> Basilica of St. Ann
> Scranton, PA 18504

Watch the Daily Mass on Television

Nationwide

Monday–Friday	3:30 p.m. EST	The Inspiration Network (INSP)
Sunday–Friday	12:30 p.m. EST	Familyland TV Network
		— available via DishNetwork
Sunday	10:00 a.m. EST	Inspirational Life Television
		(i-Lifetv) — Digital Cable

Northeastern and Central Pennsylvania

Sunday	7:00 p.m.	Catholic Television (CTV)
Monday–Friday	3:30 p.m.	Catholic Television (CTV)

Philadelphia

Monday–Friday	2:00 p.m.	WPPX – PAX61

Atlanta

Monday–Friday	9:00 a.m.	Atlanta Interfaith Broadcasters (AIB)

Weekly Novena to St. Ann on Television

Nationwide

Wednesday	9:30 a.m.	Familyland TV Network — available via DishNetwork

Northeastern and Central Pennsylvania

Sunday	6:30 p.m.	Catholic Television (CTV)
Monday	9:00 p.m.	Catholic Television (CTV)
Wednesday	11:30 a.m.	Catholic Television (CTV)

Long Island, New York

Sunday	3:00 p.m.	TELECARE
Thursday	1:00 p.m.	TELECARE
Saturday	12:00N	TELECARE

On the Web

The Daily Mass can be seen on the Internet at *www.theMass.com.*

St. Ann's Media informational site is *www.theMass.org.*

Contact 1-800-THE-MASS for specific channel information.

St. Ann Basilica Web site: *www.stannbasilica.org*

138

NOTES

1. Monastery Archives: Chronicles, 1907.
2. Ibid.
3. Ibid., 1906.
4. Ibid., 1915.
5. *La Femme Pauvre* (Paris: Mercure de France, 1927).
6. John Paul II, address to the Tribunal of the Roman Rota, January 28, 2002, *L'Osservatore Romano* (Rome), January 29, 2002.
7. Dana King, *Faith, Spirituality and Medicine* (New York: Hayworth Pastoral Press, 2000).
8. Steven Liesenseld, *On Our Pilgrimage to Eternity* (Hyde Park, N.Y.: New City Press, 2004), 57, 56; also Joseph Cardinal Ratzinger, *The Legacy of John Paul II* (San Francisco: Ignatius Press, 2005), 7.
9. *L'Osservatore Romano*, Rome, April 21, 2005.
10. Ibid.
11. Ibid.

ABOUT THE AUTHORS

Fr. Cassian Yuhaus, CP, MA, HED

After completing the Passionist novitiate and a five-year college course with a major in Philosophy, and the regular four-year course in Theology, Fr. Cassian was ordained February 27, 1951, in Union City, New Jersey. He received his Doctorate in Ecclesiastical History from the Pontifical Gregorian University, with the honor of Summa Cum Laude, and received the Papal Gold Medal for that year for Scholastic Achievement. Father studied at Munich University, Laval University, Montreal University, and Boston University working toward a second Doctorate in Comparative Religion. For twelve years he was Professor of Church History and Ecclesiology, and he was Director or Assistant Director for the Formation of Passionist seminarians.

Fr. Cassian's ministry has been global. He has worked on all continents. He is the former President of the Center for Research for the Church in Washington, D.C. He is Co-founder of the Institute for World Concerns, Duquesne University, as well as Executive Director of the Ministry for Religious Research and Consulting, Clarks Summit, Pennsylvania. He resides with other Passionist priests at the Basilica of St. Ann in Scranton, Pennsylvania.

Fr. Richard Frechette, CP, MA, DO

Fr. Richard Frechette took first vows as a Passionist in West Hartford, Connecticut, on August 17, 1975. He was ordained by Archbishop Mugavero in Jamaica, New York, on May 17, 1979. In his first five years as a priest he served as Assistant Pastor in Passionist parishes in Baltimore, Maryland, and Union City, New Jersey. He then began to fulfill the vocation he felt called to from his very first days as a Passionist: to care for the poor and destitute, especially abandoned children, orphans, and the frail elderly.

He worked alongside the famous Fr. Wasson in his orphanage in Mexico in 1994. He founded an orphanage in Honduras. He then founded two orphanages and one hospital in Haiti. Early on in Haiti, he realized these people, so poor and destitute, needed a doctor as well as a priest. He returned to New York, and after four years of intense study, he graduated with honors from the New York College of Osteopathic Medicine. He has an M.A. degree in Philosophy from Assumption College in Massachusetts and a Master's in Divinity from St. John's in New York. He continues to work by day and by night as doctor and priest among his Haitian and Honduran people.